Debunking David Barton's

JEFFERSON LIES

Debunking David Barton's

JEFFERSON LIES

Exposing the Lies of a Devout Revisionist's
Teachings in which Everything You've
Heard About Thomas Jefferson is a Myth

The Chapter That Barton Calls "LIE #2"
Jefferson Founded a Secular University

CHRIS RODDA

Published by the author
2012

ISBN-10: 1477469303
ISBN-13: 978-1477469309

Dedicated to the
REAL
Thomas Jefferson

and

to my minions,
you know who you are
and you know what you've done.

Contents

Thomas Jefferson Founded a Secular University

Barton begins the second chapter of *The Jefferson Lies* with his usual claim that "modern academics" are the revisionists and he is setting the record straight, quoting a few of these modern academics to set up the four questions he's going to answer:

1. Did Jefferson have a disdain for the influence of Christianity on education?

2. Did he found the first intentionally secular university in America?

3. Did he hire only Deists and Unitarians for his faculty?

4. Did he exclude chaplains and religious curriculum from the school?

Most Americans would probably answer "yes" to these four questions, for they have been told repeatedly by many of today's writers, both academic and journalistic, that Jefferson was an ardent secularist. But what if this is wrong?

1

What if Jefferson's own education, one that so thoroughly prepared him for the national and international scene, had been largely religious and personally satisfying to him? If such was the case then it is illogical to assert that Jefferson would seek to exclude from others that which had bene-fited him; so let's begin with a look at Jefferson's own education.

Barton then spends the next five pages describing Jefferson's own education, cleverly using some anachronisms and other mis-representations to build his case that Jefferson's own education – from his boyhood teachers through law school – was much more religious than it really was, and that this alleged religious education influenced him greatly.

Next comes an assortment of stories about Jefferson's other educational endeavors prior to the University of Virginia, which Barton claims are evidence that Jefferson promoted Christianity in schools at every possible opportunity.

Eventually, Barton gets around to the University of Virginia, where, according to him, Jefferson's own very religious education led him to establish theological schools, bring in a whole bunch of divinity professors, and do all sorts of other stuff to make sure the state university he founded was a Christian institution.

Barton ends his chapter with an unusually lengthy – nearly nine page long – examination of a letter Jefferson wrote to his nephew Peter Carr. Why the peculiar attention on this particular letter? Because of Barton's pal Glenn Beck's adoption of a phrase from this letter as his motto, which has made this letter so well known to Barton's followers that he had to come up with an explanation for it. The phrase that became Beck's motto? "Question with boldness even the existence of a God."

But we're not going to question with boldness the existence of a god here; we're just going to question with boldness the claims about Thomas Jefferson and education found in David Barton's aptly titled book, *The Jefferson Lies*.

The One About
Jefferson's Boyhood Teachers

BARTON'S LIE: Barton describes the schools of Rev. William Douglas (attended by Jefferson from 1752 until his father died in 1757) and Rev. James Fontaine Maury (attended by Jefferson from 1758 until 1760) as "religious schools," implying that these schools were part of the churches pastored by these ministers.

THE TRUTH: Many ministers of the established Anglican church in colonial Virginia ran schools on the side to make extra money. These schools provided Jefferson with what he called a "classical" education. Jefferson described Rev. Maury as "a correct classical scholar," and wrote in his autobiography what he was taught in these schools. He never mentioned religion.

> Mr. Douglas, a clergyman from Scotland, with the rudiments of the Latin and Greek languages, taught me the French; and on the death of my father, I went to the Reverend Mr. Maury, a correct classical scholar, with whom I continued two years ... [1]

Jefferson considered his second boyhood teacher, Rev. Maury, to

---

1. Albert Ellery Bergh, ed., *The Writings of Thomas Jefferson*, vol. 1, (Washington D.C.: Thomas Jefferson Memorial Association, 1907), 3.

have been adequate in teaching him the basics, but he clearly had a much lower opinion of his first teacher, Rev. Douglas. In fact, from Jefferson's autobiography and other writings, it is quite evident that his overall opinion of the clergymen in colonial Virginia was pretty low. But, more importantly, what Jefferson wrote in his autobiography clearly shows that these schools were "classical" schools. They were run by clergymen, but were separate enterprises that had nothing to do with the religious duties or churches of the clergymen who ran them. They were not "religious schools" as Barton claims. According to Jefferson:

> ... the established clergy, secure for life in their glebes and salaries, adding to these, generally, the emoluments of a classical school, found employment enough, in their farms and schoolrooms, for the rest of the week, and devoted Sunday only to the edification of their flock, by service, and a sermon at their parish church. Their other pastoral functions were little attended to. [2]

But the most interesting and telling thing that Jefferson wrote about the time period following his father's death – the period during which he was attending Rev. Maury's school – is the following, from a letter he wrote to his grandson in 1808:

> When I recollect that at fourteen years of age, the whole care and direction of myself was thrown on myself entirely, without a relation or friend qualified to advise or guide me, and recollect the various sorts of bad company with which I associated from time to time, I am astonished I did not turn off with some of them, and become as worthless to society as they were. [3]

So, where was the great influence of Rev. Maury on Jefferson's moral or religious life that Barton implies his clergymen teachers had on him? It was at age fourteen that Jefferson's father died

2. Albert Ellery Bergh, ed., *The Writings of Thomas Jefferson*, vol. 1, (Washington D.C.: Thomas Jefferson Memorial Association, 1907), 57

3. Thomas Jefferson to Thomas Jefferson Randolph, November 24, 1808. Ibid., vol. 12, 197.

and he entered Rev. Maury's school. He even boarded with this minister's family during the week, going home only on weekends. Yet he later said that he had nobody "qualified to advise or guide" him during this formative time in his life. It certainly seems from what Jefferson wrote to his grandson that Rev. Maury was merely Jefferson's teacher, and not his moral or religious adviser.

Continuing in the same letter to his grandson, Jefferson attributed the big turnaround in his life to three *non*-clergymen – his favorite professor at William and Mary, his law tutor, and a prominent politician whom he admired – all of whom he met after his time in Rev. Maury's school:

> I had the good fortune to become acquainted very early with some characters of very high standing, and to feel the incessant wish that I could ever become what they were. Under temptations and difficulties, I would ask myself what would. Dr. Small, Mr. Wythe, Peyton Randolph do in this situation? What course in it will insure me their approbation? I am certain that this mode of deciding on my conduct, tended more to correctness than any reasoning powers I possessed. Knowing the even and dignified line they pursued, I could never doubt for a moment which of two courses would be in character for them.[4]

So, based on his own words, Jefferson, after eight years in the schools of Rev. Douglas and Rev. Maury, wasn't asking himself 'what would Jesus do?,' or even 'what would his clergymen teachers do?' He was asking himself 'what would Dr. Small, Mr. Wythe, or Peyton Randolph do?'

So much for Barton's claim of the great influence Jefferson's boyhood clergymen teachers had in shaping his life.

---

4. Thomas Jefferson to Thomas Jefferson Randolph, November 24, 1808. Albert Ellery Bergh, ed., *The Writings of Thomas Jefferson,* vol. 12, (Washington D.C.: Thomas Jefferson Memorial Association, 1907), 197-198.

The One About
Jefferson and Scottish Common Sense

BARTON'S LIE: Barton claims that Jefferson and the other founders were taught Scottish Common Sense philosophy when they were students, and that Scottish Common Sense was a very religious philosophy that influenced Jefferson greatly.

THE TRUTH: The Scottish Common Sense philosophy didn't even exist yet at the time that Jefferson and virtually all of the other founders were students, so they couldn't possibly have been taught it. This philosophy wasn't published in Scotland until 1764. It was a popular philosophy in American schools in the 1800s, not the 1700s when the founders were students. It also wasn't the religious philosophy that Barton makes it out to be.

Here's how Barton skillfully constructs his Scottish Common Sense philosophy lie. He begins by simply mentioning that Dr. William Small, the professor at William and Mary whom Jefferson credited with turning his life around, was Scottish. Barton writes:

> **Scottish instructor Dr. William Small, the son of a Presbyterian minister, was Jefferson's favorite instructor. Jefferson later acknowledged: "It was my great good fortune, and what probably fixed the destinies of my life, that Dr.**

7

William Small of Scotland, was then professor."

Barton also subtly implies that there was something religious about Dr. Small by saying that his father was a minister, and by pointing out that William and Mary was a "religious school affiliated with the Anglican Church." But, although Dr. Small's father was a minister, Dr. Small himself was not. In fact, he was the only professor at William and Mary at the time that Jefferson was a student there who *wasn't* a minister, and that's who Jefferson immediately latched onto.

Barton has now planted the first seed of his lie – emphasizing the fact that Dr. Small was Scottish. He then continues:

> **Interestingly, many of the best instructors in early America were Scottish clergymen. As noted historian George Marsden affirmed, "[I]t is not much of an exaggeration to say that outside of New England, the Scots were the educators of eighteenth-century America."**

Okay, let's stop here for a minute and take a look at Barton's quote from George Marsden, who is, in fact, a noted historian who has written a number of books on religion in America. What Marsden says in his book about the Scottish influence on American education is absolutely true. Marsden, like Barton, doesn't think there's enough religion in education, but, unlike Barton, Marsden is a real historian who presents history accurately and doesn't lie to advance an agenda. What Barton does is to take a fragment of a sentence from Marsden's book out of context to fit his lie.

Here's the whole sentence from Marsden's book (emphasis mine):

> So extensive was the *Presbyterian* educational program that it is not much of an exaggeration to say that, outside of New England, the Scots were the educators of eighteenth-century America.[5]

---

5. George M. Marsden, *The Soul of the American University: From Protestant Establishment to Established Nonbelief,* (New York: Oxford University Press, 1994), 59.

See how Barton omitted the beginning of Marsden's sentence? That's because Marsden was talking about the *Presbyterian* educational program. This is the wrong denomination for Barton's story. The official church in Virginia at the time that the founders were students was, of course, the Anglican Church. Barton has just said that William and Mary was a "religious school affiliated with the Anglican Church" where "Jefferson's daily routine ... included morning and evening prayers from the Book of Common Prayer with lengthy Scripture readings" (which, of course, says absolutely nothing about whether or not Jefferson *wanted to* participate in these mandatory religious exercises). For Barton's story to work, that pesky Presbyterian part of Marsden's sentence has to go, so he just chops it off.

After misquoting Marsden, Barton continues:

These Scottish instructors regularly tutored students in what was known as the Scottish Common Sense philosophy – a method under which not only Jefferson but also other notable Virginia founding fathers were trained, including George Washington, James Madison, George Mason, Peyton Randolph, Richard Henry Lee, and Thomas Nelson.

Really? All of these founding fathers were trained in the Scottish Common Sense philosophy by their Scottish instructors? Did they have a time machine? Because that's the only way that Barton's claim could possibly be true. The Scottish Common Sense philosophy wasn't even published until 1764. With the possible exception of James Madison, who was quite a bit younger than the other founders listed by Barton, none of these founders could have been taught this philosophy in school for the simple reason that it didn't exist yet when they were in school.

In 1764, when this philosophy was first published in Scotland, Peyton Randolph was forty-three years old; George Mason was thirty-nine; George Washington and Richard Henry Lee were both thirty-two; and Thomas Nelson was twenty-six. Obviously, all five of these founders, claimed by Barton to have been taught this philosophy by their Scottish teachers, were well beyond school age by the time this philosophy was published.

So, what about Thomas Jefferson? He was twenty-one in 1764. This makes him much too old to have been trained in this philosophy by his Scottish boyhood teachers, but could he have been taught it in college by his Scottish professor William Small? Well, no. Jefferson graduated from William and Mary in 1762, two years before it was published. David Barton is either hopelessly chronologically challenged here or he's lying. I'm going with the latter.

Before going any further into the intricate web of Barton's Scottish Common Sense lie – a lie on which many of his further lies hinge – a little understanding of who a few of the Scottish Enlightenment philosophers were might be helpful, so let's get that out of the way.

Francis Hutcheson is considered the father of the Scottish Enlightenment, which began in the mid-1700s. Hutcheson's first publications came out in the late 1720s, with his major works coming out in the 1740s and 1750s. Hutcheson was a Presbyterian, but differed theologically from Presbyterians like Princeton University president John Witherspoon in that Hutcheson was a moderate (or non-evangelical) Presbyterian. As Greg Marsden explained in that same book that Barton quoted out of context earlier, Witherspoon didn't think he had to agree with Hutcheson's theology in order to accept his philosophy. Witherspoon viewed moral philosophy as a science, and, unlike most of the New England Congregationalist clergy, did not see a conflict between the science of moral philosophy and his religion.

David Hume was a secularist, whose religious beliefs would probably best be described as agnostic. He was born in 1711, and published his first work in 1739. Hume's religious beliefs (or lack thereof) caused him to be denied the Chair of Moral Philosophy at Edinburgh, although he had the support of some moderate Presbyterians. But in spite of that setback he started to become very widely read and influential in the 1740s and 1750s.

Thomas Reid, the author of the Scottish Common Sense philosophy, was a Presbyterian minister, but like Hutcheson, was a moderate Presbyterian. Although Reid was born in 1710, making him almost the same age as David Hume, he was much older when he published his work. While Hume began publishing in 1739 at the age of twenty-eight, Reid didn't publish his *Enquiry into the Human Mind on the Principles of Common Sense* until 1764, when he was fifty-four.

What needs to be kept in mind here as you read about this whole Scottish Common Sense thing is that this series of lies is really just part of Barton laying the groundwork for the whopper that he's building up to – that Thomas Jefferson rejected all of the secular Enlightenment writers, and only embraced the Christian ones. But first he needs to throw in a few more smaller lies.

For a little more reinforcement of the 'all-the-founders-were-educated-the-same-by-Scottish-clergymen-teachers' component of his story, Barton next presents an out-of-context and heavily edited quote from historian Gaillard Hunt:

> **One reason why the ruling class in Virginia acted with such unanimity [during the Revolution] … was that a large proportion of them had received the same kind of education. This usually came first from clergymen.**

What Barton is (mis)quoting here is from Hunt's *The Life of James Madison.* Barton is using this quote to bolster his contention that all of the founders had the same kind of education, even though the point that Hunt was actually making was that Madison *didn't* have the same kind of education as the other prominent founders from Virginia. Madison's early education was not from a clergyman, and he didn't go to William and Mary. As Hunt wrote, Madison's "rudimentary schooling came from a Scotchman who was not a divine."[6] But the main point that Hunt was making about the similarity of the education of these prominent founders wasn't even that it "usually first came from clergymen," which Barton presents as if

6. Gaillard Hunt, *The Life of James Madison,* (New York: Doubleday, Page & Co., 1902), 14

it were not just the main point – but the *only* point. Hunt's point was just that so many of the prominent founders from Virginia attended William and Mary, but that Madison was the oddball who didn't. Here's the beginning of the paragraph as Hunt actually wrote it:

> One reason why the ruling class in Virginia acted with such una-
> nimity in the Convention of 1776 and other crises of the Revolution
> was that a large proportion of them had received the same kind
> of education. This usually came first from clergymen of the estab-
> lished church, who added to the scanty subsistence of their livings
> by teaching. Happily, these were the better class of parsons, the
> others not having the industry or stability necessary for the task.
> From this schooling the regular course was to go to "Their
> Majesties' Royal College of William and Mary," which was one of
> the four chief colleges of the colonies, the other three being Har-
> vard, Yale and Princeton. To call the names of notable Virginians
> in the Revolution is almost to call a roll of graduates of William and
> Mary.[7]

Once he's sufficiently established in his readers' minds (with one anachronism, one deceptive implication, and two misrepresented quotes) that Jefferson and the other founders were all taught this Scottish Common Sense philosophy by their clergymen teachers, Barton presents *his* definition of what this philosophy was. According to Barton:

> **The Scottish Common Sense approach was developed by the
> Rev. Thomas Reid (1710-1796) to counter the skepticism
> of stridently secular European writers and philosophers
> such as Hume, Rousseau, Voltaire, and Malby. Reid's
> approach argued that common sense should shape philos-
> ophy rather than philosophy shaping common sense. He
> asserted that normal, everyday language could express
> philosophical principles in a way that could be understood**

---

7. Gaillard Hunt, *The Life of James Madison,* (New York: Doubleday, Page & Co., 1902), 13.

by ordinary individuals rather than just so-called elite thinkers and philosophers.

The principle tenets of Scottish Common Sense philosophy were straightforward:

1. There is a God

2. God placed into every individual a conscience – a moral sense written on his or her heart (cf. Jeremiah 31:33; Romans 2:14-15; Hebrews 8:10; 10:16; etc.)

3. God established "first principles" in areas such as law, government, education, politics, and economics, and these first principles could be discovered by the use of common sense

4. There is no conflict between reason and revelation. Both come directly from God, and revelation fortifies and clarifies reason

Where on earth Barton got these hyper-religious "principle tenets of Scottish Common Sense philosophy" from is anyone's guess, but it's obvious what he's trying to do. He needs to make the differing schools of philosophical thought a simple matter of religion vs. atheism. (Keep in mind that this is all leading up to Barton's bigger lie that Jefferson rejected all of the secular Enlightenment philosophers and only embraced the religious ones.)

Yes, the Scottish Common Sense philosophy was developed by a Christian minister, but it wasn't a religious philosophy. It was just a philosophy didn't *conflict with* religion. This philosophy was also known as Common Sense *Realism*. It was known as *realism* because it countered *idealism*. Idealism says that reality only exists as our minds perceive it. So, if our minds perceive something differently, then the thing itself is different. It's easy to see how this could conflict with religion. It would mean that if ones perception of god changes, then god himself changes, which would be unacceptable to someone who believes that god is unchangeable. Realism, on the other hand, says that things exist independently of the mind's perception of them. So, realism doesn't conflict with the Christian belief of an unchanging god. Problem solved for the Christians who wanted to get all philosophical.

To Thomas Reid, all of the idealist philosophies led to skepticism. The reason Reid thought the idealist philosophies led to skepticism was that they asserted that *some* human knowledge is impossible, therefore *all* knowledge should be doubted. Reid's Common Sense Realism counters this by saying that there are absolutes, or "first principles," that are always true and not dependent on anything else, a concept that goes all the way back to Aristotle.

Reid's 1764 work introducing his philosophy, *An Inquiry Into the Human Mind, on the Principles of Common Sense,* really didn't have anything to do with religion, other than that he had developed a philosophy that didn't conflict with his religious beliefs or pose any danger of leading to skepticism. The bulk of Reid's 1764 work was about the way in which our five senses perceive things, how our minds process the information acquired through our senses, and that this is the same for every person with all five senses intact (hence, "common" sense). The chapters of his work were titled "Of Smelling," "Of Hearing," etc.[8]

Now, we need to go back for a minute to the anachronism part of Barton's Scottish Common Sense lie. Immediately after presenting his completely religified list of what he claims were the "principle tenets" of this philosophy," Barton writes:

This is the philosophy under which Jefferson was educated at William and Mary.

Barton is now reminding his readers that Jefferson's favorite

---

8. Thomas Reid, D.D., *An Inquiry Into the Human Mind, on the Principles of Common Sense,* (London: Printer for T. Cadell, et. al., 1769).

professor at William and Mary, Dr. Small, was Scottish. But remember that book by historian George Marsden that Barton misquoted earlier? Well, Marsden actually says right there in that book that the philosophy taught by Dr. Small was that of Francis Hutcheson. Did Barton somehow just not see that Marsden very clearly said that the philosophy taught by Dr. Small was Hutcheson's while he was plucking his misquote from the same one-page long section of Marsden's book where Marsden said this?

Here's what Marsden wrote, and Barton ignored:

> Small, the only layman at the school, was professor of mathematics but also taught the moral philosophy of Francis Hutcheson. Jefferson attributed to Small his own intellectual awakening to modern science and learning.[9]

Now, as I already mentioned, Francis Hutcheson, whose philosophy Jefferson actually was taught by Dr. Small, was a moderate Presbyterian like Thomas Reid. But Hutcheson was also a great influence on the secularists David Hume and Adam Smith (best known as the author of *The Wealth of Nations*). Smith rejected Christianity and became a deist, even going as far as saying that theism might eventually disappear altogether.

But wait! John Witherspoon – the prominent Presbyterian minister and signer of the Declaration of Independence who Barton constantly holds up as the big theological influence on all the founders who went to Princeton – *also* taught the philosophy of Hutcheson, even though he disagreed with the theology of the moderate Presbyterians. Either David Barton is wrong that the differing Enlightenment philosophies were a simple matter of religion vs. atheism and secularism or the Rev. John Witherspoon was teaching a philosophy that spawned secularists and deists like Hume and Smith! I'm gonna go with David Barton being wrong.

9. George M. Marsden, *The Soul of the American University: From Protestant Establishment to Established Nonbelief*, (New York: Oxford University Press, 1994), 60.

The One About
Jefferson and Blackstone's *Commentaries*

BARTON'S LIE: A central part of Jefferson's legal education was Blackstone's *Commentaries on the Laws of England.* Jefferson approved of and liked Blackstone's *Commentaries,* which was very religious and influenced him greatly.

THE TRUTH: This is another anachronism. The first volume of Blackstone's four-volume *Commentaries* wasn't even published in England until the last year of Jefferson's law studies, so he couldn't possibly have been taught from it as a law student. And, Jefferson detested Blackstone's *Commentaries,* as evidenced by the plethora of letters he wrote saying how much he hated it.

Immediately following his easily debunked lie that Jefferson was educated under the Scottish Common Sense philosophy while at William and Mary, Barton continues:

> After completing his studies there, Jefferson entered five years of legal training with distinguished attorney and judge George Wythe, who later became a signer of the Declaration of Independence. A central subject of Jefferson's legal studies was English jurist Sir William Blackstone's four volume *Commentaries on the Laws of England* (1765-1769).

That work was an important legal textbook not only for Jefferson but for all American law students.

Like his Scottish Common Sense lie, Barton's claim that Jefferson was taught from Blackstone's *Commentaries* as a law student is an easily demonstrated anachronism. It is simply not possible for Jefferson to have been taught from Blackstone's *Commentaries* as a law student because the first volume of Blackstone's *Commentaries* wasn't even published until the last year of Jefferson's law studies. The last two volumes weren't published until Jefferson was already a practicing attorney.

Jefferson started his three years (not five years as Barton says) of law studies with George Wythe in 1762. He didn't begin practicing law until 1767, but that's not because he was a student until 1767. It was because he took some time to travel to New York and Pennsylvania in 1766 and also to do some studying of other subjects on his own before taking the bar and beginning his law practice. He did spend time in Williamsburg during the two year period from 1765 to 1767, but that wasn't because he was still a student. It was because Williamsburg was the seat of Virginia's government, where the issues that would led to the Revolution, such as the Stamp Act, were being debated in the legislature, and he wanted to be where the action was.

But even if Jefferson actually had been a student all the way up until 1767, it would still have been too early for him to have been taught from Blackstone's *Commentaries* – unless George Wythe's law instruction omitted the bulk of civil law and skipped over criminal altogether. Those were the subjects covered in the third and fourth volumes of Blackstone's, which weren't published until 1768 and 1769, when Jefferson was already a practicing attorney.

Besides Barton's anachronism, there is no question about what law texts Jefferson was really taught from. He said over and over in numerous letters that he was taught from the texts of Lord Edward Coke. Barton, of course, while claiming to get his information from Jefferson's own writings, just chooses to completely ignore what Jefferson himself actually said in all those letters.

So, why would Barton even want to lie about what law texts Jefferson was taught from? Well, because there are many parts of Blackstone's *Commentaries* that are really, really religious.

The next step of Barton's Blackstone's lie is to make it appear that Jefferson was not only taught from these hyper-religious law books, but that he highly approved of them and thought that the popularity of Blackstone's among American lawyers was a good thing. How Barton accomplishes this building block of his lie is to misrepresent something that Jefferson wrote about Blackstone's by taking it completely out of context. According to Barton:

Jefferson affirmed that American lawyers used *Blackstone's* with the same dedication and reverence that Muslims used the Koran.

Wow! Sounds like Jefferson must have really thought it was great that so many American lawyers were using Blackstone's, right? Wrong! Barton is misrepresenting Jefferson's comment about Blackstone's from an 1810 letter he wrote to Judge John Tyler (the father of the future president). Jefferson was saying that the use of Blackstone's by American lawyers was a *bad* thing. Here's what he actually wrote, restored to the context that Barton removed it from:

I have long lamented with you the depreciation of law science. The opinion seems to be that Blackstone is to us what the Alcoran is to the Mahometans, that everything which is necessary is in him, and what is not in him is not necessary. I still lend my counsel and books to such young students as will fix themselves in the neighborhood. Coke's institutes and reports are their first, and Blackstone their last book, after an intermediate course of two or three years. It is nothing more than an elegant digest of what they will then have acquired from the real fountains of the law.[10]

10. Thomas Jefferson to John Tyler, May 26, 1810. Albert Ellery Bergh, ed., *The Writings of Thomas Jefferson*, vol. 12, (Washington D.C.: Thomas Jefferson Memorial Association, 1907), 392-393.

In Barton's book, Blackstone's is presented as another religious Enlightenment era influence on Jefferson. (Remember, we are *still* building up to Barton's big lie that Jefferson embraced all the religious Enlightenment writers and rejected the secular ones.) But Blackstone's was a law text, or, to be more specific, a digest of the laws of England.

Jefferson of course didn't think that any of the religious laws of England found in Blackstone's, such as those found in its section on "Offenses Against God and Religion," should be part of American law. That goes without saying. But Jefferson's two biggest problems with Blackstone's actually had nothing to do its religious content. Barton, of course, makes this all about religion, as we'll see in a minute when we get to what Barton quotes from Blackstone's in *The Jefferson Lies,* as well as his reason for quoting it. But first, let's take a look at a few more of Jefferson's letters about Blackstone's.

As I said, Jefferson wrote many letters about Blackstone's. The ones I've chosen here were selected to kill all the birds with one stone. First, they leave no doubt that Jefferson did not like Blackstone's one bit; second, they clearly show that Jefferson did not want Blackstone's used as a law text at the University of Virginia; and, third, they explain what Jefferson's non-religious reasons were for not wanting Blackstone's to be used in America.

The first of Jefferson's non-religious reasons for not liking Blackstone's was that he just didn't consider it to be very instructive for law students. The reason that Blackstone's had become so popular among law students was that it was much easier reading than the texts that previous generations had learned from. Jefferson, who often advised and mentored young law students, wouldn't even let them read Blackstone's until after they had already learned the law from the texts that he himself had used as a student. Jefferson's opinion was that reading Blackstone's led students to think they knew a lot more than they actually did, as he wrote in 1812 in another letter to John Tyler.

A student finds there a smattering of everything, and his indolence easily persuades him that if he understands that book, he is master of the whole body of the law. The distinction between these, and those who have drawn their stores from the deep and rich mines of Coke on Littleton, seems well understood even by the unlettered common people, who apply the appellation of Blackstone lawyers to these ephemeral insects of the law.[11]

The second, and more important, reason that Jefferson disapproved of Blackstone's was that it contained British principles that were incompatible with, and even dangerous to, the republican principles of American government. The use of Blackstone's as a primary textbook was part of Jefferson's overall concern about what was being taught in America's colleges in the early 1800s, particularly in the Northern states, where the lawyers who were teaching the next generation of lawyers had been among the pro-British Federalists in the 1790s who had always favored hanging on to the aristocratic customs of England and other anti-American ideas that were glorified by Blackstone.

Jefferson wrote about this in an 1814 letter to Horatio Spafford, who had just published *A Gazetteer of the State of New York*. Spafford had noted that, in his state, the undesireable British principles that had never ceased to exist among the merchants and the clergy had also crept into the law profession. In his letter to Spafford, one of the influences Jefferson blamed for this troubling trend among American lawyers was Blackstone.

They [lawyers] have, in the Mother country, been generally the firmest supporters of the free principles of their constitution. But there too they have changed. I ascribe much of this to the substitution of Blackstone for my Lord Coke, as an elementary work. In truth, Blackstone and Hume have made tories of all England, and are making tories of those young Americans whose native feelings of independence do not place them above the wily sophistries of a Hume or a Blackstone. These two books, but especially the former,

11. Thomas Jefferson to John Tyler, June 17, 1812. Albert Ellery Bergh, ed., *The Writings of Thomas Jefferson,* vol. 13, (Washington D.C.: Thomas Jefferson Memorial Association, 1907), 166-167.

have done more towards the suppression of the liberties of man, than all the million of men in arms of Bonaparte and the millions of human lives with the sacrifice of which he will stand loaded before the judgment seat of his Maker. I fear nothing for our liberty from the assaults of force; but I have seen and felt much, and fear more from English books, English prejudices, English manners, and the apes, the dupes, and designs among our professional crafts.[12]

Since the popularity of Blackstone's *Commentaries* was mainly due to its readability and arrangement, and not its content, Jefferson was quite pleased when a more readable edition of Coke's *Institutes of the Lawes of England*, the primary text that he had been taught from, was published by J. H. Thomas in 1818. He was also pleased when he heard in 1825 that Francis Gilmer, who was going to be the law professor at the University of Virginia, had chosen Thomas's edition of Coke's *Institutes* as his textbook.

I am very glad to find from a conversation with Mr. Gilmer, that he considers Coke Littleton, as methodized by Thomas, as unquestionably the best elementary work, and the one which will be the text-book of his school. It is now as agreeable reading as Blackstone, and much more profound.[13]

But Francis Gilmer did not end up becoming the University of Virginia's law professor. Gilmer became ill in the fall of 1825, and died in February 1826, the month he was supposed to begin teaching, so Jefferson and James Madison, who was a member of the university's Board of Visitors, had to find a replacement.

There is no question from the letter that Jefferson wrote to Madison at this time that he absolutely did not want Blackstone's *Commentaries,* or even any law professor who was influenced by

12. Thomas Jefferson to Horatio G. Spafford, March 17, 1814. Albert Ellery Bergh, ed., *The Writings of Thomas Jefferson,* vol. 14, (Washington D.C.: Thomas Jefferson Memorial Association, 1907), 119-120.
13. Thomas Jefferson to unknown recipient, October 25, 1825. Ibid., vol. 16, 128-129.

Blackstone's *Commentaries,* at his university.

> In the selection of our Law professor, we must be rigorously atten-
> tive to his political principles. You will recollect that before the
> Revolution, Coke Littleton was the universal elementary book of
> law students, and a sounder Whig never wrote, nor of profounder
> learning in the orthodox doctrines of the British constitution, or in
> what were called English liberties. You remember also that our
> lawyers were then all Whigs. But when his black-letter text, and
> uncouth, but cunning learning got out of fashion, and the honeyed
> Mansfieldism of Blackstone became the students' hornbook, from
> that moment, that profession (the nursery of our Congress) began
> to slide into toryism, and nearly all the young brood of lawyers now
> are of that hue. They suppose themselves, indeed, to be Whigs,
> because they no longer know what Whigism or republicanism
> means. It is in our seminary that vestal flame is to be kept alive; it is
> thence it is to spread anew over our own and the sister States. If
> we are true and vigilant in our trust, within a dozen or twenty years
> a majority of our own legislature will be from one school, and many
> disciples will have carried its doctrines home with them to their
> several States, and will have leavened thus the whole mass.[14]

Then there's this dig at "Blackstone lawyers" in an 1811 letter
from Jefferson to William Cabell Rives, one of the many students
whom Jefferson advised on their education.

> Nothing can be sounder than your view of the importance of
> laying a broad foundation in other branches of knolege whereon
> to raise the superstructure of any particular science which one
> would chuse to profess with credit & usefulness. The lamentable
> disregard of this since the revolution has filled our country with
> Blackstone lawyers, Sangrado physicians, a ranting clergy, &

---

14. Thomas Jefferson to James Madison, February 17, 1826. James Morton Smith, ed.,
*The Republic of Letters: The Correspondence Between Thomas Jefferson and James Madison
1776-1826,* vol. 3, (New York and London: W.W. Norton & Company, 1995), 1965.

a lounging gentry, who render neither honor nor service to mankind...[15]

Every single letter that Jefferson ever wrote about Blackstone's says the same thing – Jefferson did not like Blackstone's. So, how could David Barton, who claims to have read all of Jefferson's original writings, have missed this? The answer is that he couldn't have. Barton is deliberately lying and intentionally misrepresenting the one letter that he cites.

And now, unfortunately, we've just gone around in a big circle and are coming back to that blasted Scottish Common Sense stuff again, this time for Barton to say that Sir William Blackstone was *also* influenced by this philosophy. According to Barton:

In this indispensable legal text, Blackstone forcefully expounded the four prime tenets of Scottish Common Sense philosophy:

Man, considered as a creature, must necessarily be subject to the laws of his Creator.... This will of his maker is called the law of nature.... These are the eternal, immutable laws of good and evil, to which the Creator Himself in all His dispensations conforms, and which He has enabled human reason to discover, so far as they are necessary for the conduct of human actions.... And if our reason were always...clear and perfect,...the task would be pleasant and easy; we should need no other guide but this. But every man now finds the contrary in his own experience: that his reason is corrupt, and his understanding full of ignorance and error. This has given manifold occasion for the benign inter-

---

15. Thomas Jefferson to William Cabell Rives, September 18, 1811. *The Thomas Jefferson Papers Series 1, General Correspondence, 1651-1827,* Library of Congress Manuscript Division.

position of Divine Providence; which ... hath been pleased at sundry times and in divers manners to discover and enforce its laws by an immediate and direct revelation. The doctrines thus delivered we call the revealed or Divine law, and they are to be found only in the Holy Scriptures. ... Upon these two foundations, the law of nature and the law of revelation, depend all human laws; that is to say, no human laws should be suffered to contradict these.

What Barton quotes here is actually a whole bunch of sentences and phrases from four pages of the first volume of Blackstone's, strung together to fit what *he* claims were the four tenets of Scottish Common Sense philosophy so he can claim that Blackstone's "expounded" this philosophy. Once again, however, we have a bit of a timing problem. Although the first volume of Blackstone's *Commentaries* wasn't published until 1766, two years after Reid published his Scottish Common Sense philosophy, there are really no new ideas in what Barton quotes here from Blackstone's *Commentaries* that Blackstone hadn't previously presented in his earlier published works, and those works *do* predate the 1764 publication of Reid's philosophy. All that was "expounded" in this section of Blackstone's *Commentaries* quoted by Barton was what Blackstone himself had written in his own 1756 work, *An Analysis of the laws of England*, which predated Reid's Scottish Common Sense philosophy by about eight years.

Barton then follows his quote from Blackstone's – which he has just told his readers was an expounding of Reid's Scottish Common Sense philosophy – with:

The same four Scottish Common Sense tenets were subsequently included by Jefferson in the Declaration of Independence.

So, the hyper-religious Blackstone's *Commentaries*, which Jefferson not only hated, but was somehow taught from even though he was nearly finished with his law studies by the time its first volume was published, somehow influenced Jefferson's writing of the Declaration of Independence, all somehow via Reid's Scottish Common Sense philosophy, of course. Oddly, Jefferson never mentioned any of this when *he* wrote about where the ideas in the Declaration came from.

The One About
Jefferson Rejecting Secular Enlightenment Writers

BARTON'S LIE: Jefferson rejected all of the secular Enlightenment writers and embraced only the religious ones.

THE TRUTH: There were some secular Enlightenment writers whom Jefferson didn't like, but his reasons for disliking them had absolutely nothing to do with their secularism or religious opinions.

As I've already mentioned, all of Barton's Scottish Common Sense mumbo-jumbo was just building up to his bigger lie – that Jefferson rejected all of the secular Enlightenment writers and embraced only the religious ones. Here's where he starts to pull it all together:

> **Even though Jefferson's own personal education at the elementary, secondary, and postsecondary levels consistently incorporated religious instruction, today's writers repeatedly insist that it was the secular European Enlightenment rather than Scottish Common Sense that was the greatest influence on Jefferson's thinking.**

He then goes on to say:

> **Far too many of today's writers, consumed by the spirit of**

Academic Collectivism, regularly regurgitate each other's claims that Jefferson's philosophy and the Declaration were products of the secular European Enlightenment. Yet Jefferson himself forcefully disagreed, and when some in his day had suggested that he based the Declaration on the writings of other philosophers, he responded, "[W]hether I had gathered my ideas from reading or reflection I do not know. I know only that I turned to neither book or pamphlet while writing it."

What Barton completely ignores here is that Jefferson actually *did* say what he was accused of copying when he wrote the Declaration – John Locke's *Second Treatise on Government* and a pamphlet written by James Otis of Massachusetts that *cited* John Locke's *Second Treatise on Government*. Jefferson also stated quite clearly, as we'll see in a minute, which philosophers the ideas for the Declaration actually did come from. But, not being one to let what Jefferson actually wrote stand in his way, Barton continues:

In fact, he specifically asserted that the Declaration of Independence was "an expression of the *American* mind" (emphasis added) rather than a lexicon of European ideas.

What Jefferson meant when he said that the Declaration was "an expression of the American mind" was that it was based on ideas that Americans had already embraced from the writings of Americans like James Otis – whose ideas did, in fact, come from a *European* Enlightenment philosopher.

The pamphlet by James Otis that Jefferson was accused of copying when he wrote the Declaration was titled "A Vindication of the Conduct of the House of Representatives, of the Province of Massachusetts Bay." It was written by Otis in 1762 in response to the British government's starting to do the kind of things that would eventually lead to the Revolution. Otis's pamphlet was prompted by an early instance of "taxation without representation" in what would become the long list of objectionable taxes and laws that would be imposed by the British to make Americans pay the British debt for the French and Indian War. This particular pamphlet, which Jefferson said he had never read, really was extremely similar to the Declaration of Independence, but so were lots of other things that Jefferson would have read in the years leading up to the writing of the Declaration. What Otis cited as the basis for the ideas he expressed in his 1762 pamphlet was John Locke's *Second Treatise on Government*. From that point on, Locke's ideas became a mainstay in the writings of pretty much everyone else – John Adams, Samuel Adams, James Wilson, and many others. By the time Jefferson wrote the Declaration, Locke's ideas had *become* the "expression of the American mind" that Jefferson was referring to.

Jefferson's response to his critics, that he hadn't referred to any book or pamphlet while writing the Declaration, is entirely believable. He wouldn't have needed to refer to what anyone else had written. He knew exactly what others had been writing and saying in the years leading up to the Declaration, and knew exactly where these new "American" ideas had come from. Here's what Jefferson actually said in the letter that Barton quotes:

> Neither aiming at originality of principle or sentiment, nor yet copied from any particular and previous writing, it was intended to be an expression of the American mind, and to give to that expression the proper tone and spirit called for by the occasion. All its authority rests then on the harmonizing sentiments of the day, whether expressed in conversation, in letters, printed essays, or in the elementary books of public right, as Aristotle, Cicero, Locke, Sidney, etc. [16]

If Barton read the letter in which Jefferson wrote all of this (which he must have read to have plucked out the snippet that he quotes), how could he possibly have missed the part where Jefferson actually

---

16. Thomas Jefferson to Henry Lee, May 8, 1825. Albert Ellery Bergh, ed., *The Writings of Thomas Jefferson,* vol. 16, (Washington D.C.: Thomas Jefferson Memorial Association, 1907), 118-119.

named the philosophers who he thought had influenced the "American mind?" Jefferson said this in the very next sentence after the one that Barton plucks his quotes from. But Barton, of course, needs to omit that Jefferson actually said the sources of the ideas in the "American mind" were European philosophers like Locke and Sidney and ancient philosophers like Aristotle and Cicero because that would conflict with his claim that the ideas in the Declaration came from his hyper-religious version of Thomas Reid's Scottish Common Sense philosophy, apparently somehow via Blackstone – which in itself contradicts what Barton himself is claiming since both Reid and Blackstone were Europeans.

Barton then quickly turns around and obfuscates the contradiction in his American ideas vs. European ideas claim by saying that he's *not* saying that the European Enlightenment writers had no influence on the founders. He's just saying that it was "primarily the Christian writers, not the secular ones, upon which Jefferson and the other Founders relied."

If you're really confused at this point, don't worry; it's not you. Barton just *somehow* had to get from that Scottish Common Sense to the bigger lie he's been building up to, and he's almost there.

Barton next cites a study[17] that determined that the four most frequently cited Enlightenment writers during the founding era were Montesquieu, Blackstone, Locke, and Hume, making a point to note that Hume was the only secularist of the four. He then asks:

But if the Founders relied primarily on Christian thinkers rather than secular thinkers, then why was Hume the fourth most cited?

And then, answering his own question, he writes:

Because the Founders regularly cited him in order to *refute* his political theories rather than endorse them.

17. For a full explanation of how the results of this study, conducted by Donald S. Lutz of the University of Houston, are misrepresented by Barton to make it appear that the Bible was the source most cited by the founders, see http://www.talk2action.org/story/2007/4/15/04011/4130.

What Barton does here is to use two examples of secular Enlightenment writers whom Jefferson didn't like – David Hume and Abbé Raynal – and then claim that because Jefferson didn't like these two particular secularist writers, he rejected *all* of the secular Enlightenment writers and was only influenced by the Christian ones.

Now, it is completely true that Jefferson didn't like either Hume or Raynal, but, as we'll see, Jefferson's dislike of these two writers had absolutely nothing to do with their secularism or religious opinions. Barton just takes some things Jefferson wrote about these two writers out of context (in one case inconceivably out of context, even for Barton) to make it appear that their secularism and religious opinions were the reasons Jefferson didn't like them.

Here's what Barton says about Jefferson's opinion of Hume:

If Jefferson was indeed antireligious, then perhaps he would be drawn toward Hume as a kindred spirit. Such was definitely not the case. To the contrary, Jefferson found Hume "endeavoring to mislead, by either the suppression of a truth or by giving it a false covering." He even regretted the early influence that Hume had once had upon him, candidly lamenting:

> **I remember well the enthusiasm with which I devoured it [Hume's work] when young, and the length of time, the research, and reflection which were necessary to eradicate the poison it had instilled into my mind.**

In reality, the problem that Jefferson had with David Hume had absolutely nothing to do with religion. Jefferson's problem with Hume was that he was an historical revisionist. That's what he was writing about in that quote that Barton takes out of context.

Remember that letter back in the section about Blackstone where Jefferson said that the "wily sophistries" of Blackstone were turning young Americans into Tories? Well, if you recall, Jefferson was talking about *both* Hume and Blackstone in that letter.

> Blackstone and Hume have made tories of all England, and are making tories of those young Americans whose native feelings of independence do not place them above the wily sophistries of a Hume or a Blackstone.[18]

Just as Jefferson was worried about the danger of Blackstone's *Commentaries* being such a popular textbook for American law students, he worried for the same reason about Hume's six-volume work, *The History of England,* being what American students were learning British history from.

Because Hume's *History of England* had been around since the days when Jefferson himself was still a student, he knew from his own experience that he'd been sucked into believing that it was a true and accurate history when he was young. It wasn't until he was older that Jefferson realized that Hume was revising history to advance a pro-monarchy agenda. That's what Jefferson was talking about when he said Hume was "endeavoring to mislead, by either the suppression of a truth or by giving it a false covering." He was talking about Hume distorting history – you know, like David Barton does.

Where Barton gets his out-of-context quote from is an 1810 letter that Jefferson wrote to publisher William Duane about John Baxter's *A New and Impartial History of England.* What Baxter had done was to take Hume's *History of England*, correct all of the inaccuracies and lies in it, and publish it as a new "impartial" edition. Jefferson was obviously very happy about this.

Here's the whole letter from Jefferson to William Duane that Barton plucks his out-of-context quote from:

> I have been long intending to write to you as one of the associated company for printing useful works.

---

18. Thomas Jefferson to Horatio G. Spafford, March 17, 1814. Albert Ellery Bergh, ed., *The Writings of Thomas Jefferson,* vol. 14, (Washington D.C.: Thomas Jefferson Memorial Association, 1907), 120.

Our laws, language, religion, politics and manners are so deeply laid in English foundations, that we shall never cease to consider their history as a part of ours, and to study ours in that as its origin. Every one knows that judicious matter and charms of style have rendered Hume's history the manual of every student. I remember well the enthusiasm with which I devoured it when young, and the length of time, the research and reflection which were necessary to eradicate the poison it had instilled into my mind. It was unfortunate that he first took up the history of the Stuarts, became their apologist, and advocated all their enormities. To support his work, when done, he went back to the Tudors, and so selected and arranged the materials of their history as to present their arbitrary acts only, as the genuine samples of the constitutional power of the crown, and, still writing backwards, he then reverted to the early history, and wrote the Saxon and Norman periods with the same perverted view. Although all this is known, he still continues to be put into the hands of all our young people, and to infect them with the poison of his own principles of government. It is this book which has undermined the free principles of the English government, has persuaded readers of all classes that these were usurpations on the legitimate and salutary rights of the crown, and has spread universal toryism over the land. And the book will still continue to be read here as well as there. Baxter, one of Horne Tooke's associates in persecution, has hit on the only remedy the evil admits. He has taken Hume's work, corrected in the text his misrepresentations, supplied the truths which he suppressed, and yet has given the mass of the work in Hume's own words. And it is wonderful how little interpolation has been necessary to make it a sound history, and to justify what should have been it's title, to wit, "Hume's history of England abridged and rendered faithful to fact and principle."[19]

19. Thomas Jefferson to William Duane, August 12, 1810. Albert Ellery Bergh, ed., *The Writings of Thomas Jefferson,* vol. 12, (Washington D.C.: Thomas Jefferson Memorial Association, 1907), 405-406.

Barton then proceeds to do the same thing with Abbé Raynal, his second example of a secular Enlightenment writer whom Jefferson criticized, writing:

Jefferson was similarly forthright in his criticism of other secular enlightenment writers, including Guillaume Thomas François Raynal (known as Abbé Raynal). Jefferson described his works as "a mass of errors and misconceptions from beginning to end," containing "a great deal of falsehood" and being "wrong exactly in the same proportion." He even described Raynal as "a mere shrimp."

As with Hume, Jefferson's problem with Raynal had nothing to do with religion. The first two snippets that Barton quotes from Jefferson – the ones about Raynal's work – were about a particular work. Raynal had written a history of the American Revolution that was full of errors, and these errors had been copied from Raynal's book into another work.

But it's the last snippet of a quote that Barton uses – that Jefferson called Raynal "a mere shrimp" – that really shows Barton's astounding level of dishonesty and just how far he will go in taking things out of context. The "mere shrimp" comment not only had nothing to do with religion; it didn't even have anything to do with Raynal's writings. It was referring to the man's height!

Besides the problem with his bad history of the American Revolution, Jefferson and Benjamin Franklin, who knew Raynal in Paris, just personally did not like this guy. Again, this had absolutely nothing to do with his secularism or religious opinions. The reason they didn't like him was that he was always putting down Americans, claiming that Americans were both physically and mentally inferior to Europeans. The "mere shrimp" comment actually comes from a story told by Franklin about how he put Raynal in his place at a dinner party in France.

In 1818, author and publisher Robert Walsh was writing an article about Franklin. Walsh wrote to Jefferson, asking him if he had any good Franklin anecdotes. Jefferson wrote back to Walsh, recounting two anecdotes that he had heard from Franklin. Here is the one that the "mere shrimp" comment comes from:

> The Doctor told me, at Paris, the two following anecdotes of Abbe Raynal. He had a party to dine with him one day at Passy of whom one half were Americans, the other half French & among the last was the Abbe. During the dinner he got on his favorite theory of the degeneracy of animals and even of man, in America, and urged it with his usual eloquence. The Doctor at length noticing the accidental stature and positions of his guests, at table, 'Come' says he, 'M. L'Abbe, let us try this question by the fact before us. We are here one half Americans, & one half French, and it happens that the Americans have placed themselves on one side of the table, and our French friends are on the other. Let both parties rise and we will see on which side nature has degenerated.' It happened that his American guests were Carmichael, Harmer, Humphreys and others of the finest stature and form, while those of the other side were remarkably diminutive, and the Abbe himself particularly was a mere shrimp. He parried the appeal however, by a complimentary admission of exceptions, among which the Doctor himself was a conspicuous one. [20]

Yes, my friends, *that* is how far David Barton is willing to go with his misquotes – claiming that a comment about someone's height was a "vehement denunciation" by Thomas Jefferson of the religious opinions in that person's writings!

With his two examples of Hume and Raynal – both of which are complete misrepresentations of what Jefferson wrote – Barton now proceeds as if he has proved that Jefferson was not influenced by *any* secular Enlightenment writers:

So if secular Enlightenment writers were not a primary force in shaping Jefferson's thinking, then who was? Jefferson

20. Thomas Jefferson to Robert Walsh, December 4, 1818. Paul Leicester Ford, ed., *The Works of Thomas Jefferson,* vol. 12, (New York: G.P. Putnam's Sons, 1905), 110-111.

himself answered that question, declaring that "Bacon, Newton and Locke… [are] my Trinity of the three greatest men the world had ever produced."

Barton then proceeds to explain that the reason Jefferson admired and was influenced so much by Francis Bacon, Isaac Newton, and John Locke was because of their theological writings.

The One About
Jefferson and Bacon, Newton, and Locke

BARTON'S LIE: John Locke's political works were a *religious* influence on Jefferson because in his *Treatises of Government* "Locke
invoked the Bible over 1,500 times." Therefore, the Declaration of
Independence was a religious document.

THE TRUTH: John Locke "invoked" the Bible over 1,500 times in
his *Treatises of Government* because he was arguing against someone who had used biblical arguments to justify the divine right of
kings. Since he was arguing against biblical arguments, he of course
invoked the Bible a lot. To arrive at his astounding number of over
1,500 Bible invocations, Barton counts things such as every instance
of Locke's making a reference to "Adam," which alone account for
hundreds of what Barton classifies as invocations of the Bible. But
Locke's hundreds of references to "Adam" were simply because he
used the name "Adam" throughout his work as a literary device to
mean the origin of the divinely appointed line of monarchs.

Before getting to what Barton says about Locke, we need to get
what he says about the other two members of Jefferson's trinity of
"greatest men" out of the way. Locke is, of course, the most important of the three when discussing Jefferson's political influences,
but Barton also has a few lies in his book about the other two.

Barton begins by pointing out that Bacon, Newton, and Locke all wrote theological works. This is true. They all did. But this doesn't mean that it was their theological works that made Jefferson consider them the three greatest men who ever lived.

The reason given by Jefferson for his choice of Bacon, Newton, and Locke as the three greatest men who ever lived was that they had "laid the foundation of those superstructures which have been raised in the Physical and Moral sciences,"[21] not that they were his favorite theologians. Barton is just once again making something all about religion that wasn't all about religion.

First of all, it is impossible for Jefferson to have even read Newton's theological writings because almost none of them had been published at the time that Jefferson was alive. There was one book on church history, and one on the Apocalypse, but the rest of Newton's "1.3 million words on Biblical subjects" that Barton writes about didn't come to light until over a century after Jefferson's death, when they were auctioned off in 1936 by someone who had inherited them. Barton very deliberately hides this inconvenient little fact by chopping it out of the article he quotes about Newton's theological writings, replacing the words "Yet this vast legacy lay hidden from public view for two centuries until the auction of his nonscientific writings in 1936"[22] with an ellipsis.

The reason that Newton's theological writings weren't published at the same time that his scientific papers were published was that they were rejected by Cambridge University because of Newton's heretical religious views. All that diligent studying of the Bible that Newton did had apparently turned him into a Unitarian, rejecting the Christian doctrine of the trinity and everything else that he considered irrational and superstitious (pretty much the same opinions that Jefferson later independently arrived at from his own study of the Bible).

Barton also points out Francis Bacon's theological works, but I

---

21. Thomas Jefferson to John Ttrumbull, February 15, 1789. Julian P. Boyd, ed., *The Papers of Thomas Jefferson*, vol. 14, (Princeton, NJ: Princeton University Press, 1958), 561.

22. Charles E. Hummel, "The Faith Behind the Famous: Isaac Newton," *ChristianHistory.net*, April 1, 1991. http://www.christianitytoday.com/ch/1991/issue30/3038.html. Accessed 9/1/12.

think it's a pretty safe bet that it was Bacon's contributions to science, law, ethics, and history, rather than his theological works, that caused Jefferson to hold him in such high esteem. Jefferson's writings show that he often recommended Bacon's works on science, law, and history, not his theological works.

But, as I said, it is Locke who needs to be given the most attention here, because it was Locke who played the biggest role in influencing Jefferson, as well as many of the other founders, in their principles of government.

Barton begins his section on Locke:

Today's writers describe Locke as a deist (or at least a follower of an early form of deism), but historians of earlier generations described him as a Christian theologian.

Barton then goes on to list a bunch of Locke's religious writings, describing three of them like this:

And when antireligionists attacked Christianity, Locke defended it in his book *The Reasonableness of Christianity as Delivered in the Scriptures* (1695). When attacks continued, Locke responded with *A Vindication of The Reasonableness of Christianity* (1695), and then with *A Second Vindication of The Reasonableness of Christianity* (1697).

Seriously, Mr. Barton? John Locke was defending Christianity against *antireligionists*? Locke's vindications of his *Reasonableness of Christianity* were written in response to a prominent Calvinist minister, not an antireligionist!

Here's how it went down:

In 1695, Locke published his *Reasonableness of Christianity*. He published this book anonymously (you know, because it was the orthodox Christian theologians who had to publish their works anonymously in 17th century England).

John Edwards, a lecturer at Trinity Church, Cambridge, minister of St. Sepulchre's Church, Cambridge, and author of numerous theological works (you know, your typical *antireligionist*), refuted Locke's book in a book titled *Some Thoughts concerning the several Causes and Occasions of Atheism, especially in the Present Age, with some brief Reflections on Sociniunism and on a late Book entituled "The Reasonableness of Christianity as delivered in the Scriptures,"* also published in 1695.

Locke (still writing anonymously) then shot back at Edwards with *A Vindication of The Reasonableness of Christianity, from Mr. Edwards's Reflections*, the first two sentences of which were:

> My Book had not been long out, before it fell under the correction of the author of a Treatise, entitled, "Some Thoughts concerning the several Causes and Occasions of Atheism, especially in the present Age." No contemptible adversary, I'll assure you; since, as it seems, he has got the faculty to heighten every thing that displeases him, into the capital crime of atheism; and breathes against those, who come in his way, a pestilential air, whereby every the least distemper is turned into the plague, and becomes mortal. [23]

Edwards then shot back at Locke in 1696 with *Socinianism Unmask'd. A discourse shewing the unreasonableness of a late writer's opinion concerning the necessity of only one article of Christian faith; and of his other assertions in his late book, entituled, The Reasonableness of Christianity as Deliver'd in the Scriptures, and in his vindication of it.*

Locke then shot back at Edwards with *A Second Vindication of The Reasonableness of Christianity, &c.*

But, in David Barton's story, Locke is a Christian theologian who was defending Christianity against *antireligionists,* because that's who Barton needs him to be. Locke can't have been someone who was accused by the clergy of his own day of being a Socinian (an anti-trinitarian, but with a few differences from Unitarians). In Barton's story, it is "today's writers" who have come up with this

---

23. *The Works of John Locke,* vol. 6, (London: C. and J. Rivington, et. al., 1824), 160.

crazy notion that Locke wasn't the devout, orthodox Christian that Barton needs him to have been. Therefore, he just erases from history that it was the clergy of Locke's own time who first accused him of being a heretic.

And, you know who else wrote stuff criticizing Locke? Rev. Thomas Reid, the guy who developed that good old Scottish Common Sense philosophy!

Anyway, after naming a bunch of Locke's theological works, Barton continues:

Furthermore, in his *Two Treatises of Government* (1689) – the work specifically relied upon by Jefferson and the other Founders as they drafted the Declaration – Locke invoked the Bible over 1,500 times.

Wait a minute! I thought the Declaration of Independence was based on Scottish Common Sense philosophy via Blackstone's *Commentaries!* Now he's saying it was Locke? History is so confusing when you're reading David Barton's version of it!

As I already mentioned, those 1,500 Bible *invocations* in Locke's *Two Treatises of Government* are there because Locke was arguing against the biblical arguments used by Sir Robert Filmer to defend the divine right of kings in his 1680 work *Patriarcha; or the Natural Power of Kings*. Obviously, Locke would have had a pretty hard time arguing against Filmer's biblical arguments without invoking the Bible. So, between quoting Filmer and rebutting Filmer's arguments (which was the entire purpose of Locke's first *Treatise*), those Bible invocations added up pretty quickly. There are about five hundred references to Adam alone just because of Filmer's argument that the "Lordship which *Adam* by Command had over the whole World, and by Right descending from him the *Patriarchs* did enjoy, was as large and ample as the Absolutest Dominion of any *Monarch* which hath been since the Creation."[24]

24. Sir Robert Filmer, *Patriarcha; of the Natural Power of Kings,* (London: Richard Chiswell, 1680), 13.

Since the basis of Filmer's argument was that the divine right of kings began with Adam and continued with his biblical successors and was therefore mandated by the Bible, Locke repeatedly referred back to this basis of Filmer's arguments in chapters with titles like "Of Adam's Title To Sovereignty By Fatherhood," which began:

> There is one thing more, and then I think I have given you all that our author [Robert Filmer] brings for proof of Adam's sovereignty, and that is a supposition of a natural right of dominion over his children, by being their father: and this title of fatherhood he is so pleased with, that you will find it brought in almost in every page; particularly he says, not only Adam, but the succeeding patriarchs had by right of fatherhood royal authority over their children, p. 12. And in the same page, this subjection of children being the fountain of all regal authority, &c. This being, as one would think by his so frequent mentioning it, the main basis of all his frame, we may well expect clear and evident reason for it, since he lays it down as a position necessary to his purpose, that every man that is born is so far from being free, that by his very birth he becomes a subject of him that begets him, O[bservations] 156. so that Adam being the only man created, and all ever since being begotten, no body has been born free.[25]

As you can see, Locke used the name Adam three times in just this single paragraph in this one chapter. Locke made constant references like this to Adam, as well as the "succeeding patriarchs" from the Bible, throughout his work in the course of rebutting Filmer's argument that Adam and Adam's successors were all made sovereign by God. As Locke himself said of this argument in the paragraph I just quoted, "you will find it brought in almost in every page" of Filmer's work. Naturally, therefore, Locke also had to bring it up in one way or another in almost every page of *his* work. This meant repeatedly using the name Adam and other names from the

25. *The Works of John Locke,* vol. 4, (London: C. and J. Rivington, et. al., 1824), 249-250.

Bible. If you go and count every one of these references to biblical names and biblical events as an instance of Locke's "invoking the Bible," then he certainly did invoke the Bible over 1,500 times.

But Barton knows that his readers aren't actually going to go and read Locke's *Treatises of Government* to see for themselves what these 1,500 biblical references really were. They're just going to parrot his talking point that there are over 1,500 references to the Bible in Locke's *Treatises of Government*, just like he wants them to.

Barton continues:

Jefferson studied not only Locke's governmental and legal writings but also his theological texts. His own personal summation of Locke's view of Christianity clearly shows that he definitely did not consider Locke to be a deist. According to Jefferson:

Locke's system of Christianity is this: Adam was created happy & immortal. ... By sin he lost this so that he became subject to total death (like that of brutes[animals]) to the crosses & unhappiness of this life. At the intercession however of the son of god this sentence was in part remitted. ... And moreover to them who believed their faith was to be counted for righteousness [Romans 4:3, 5]. Not that faith without works was to save them; St. James. c. 2. sais expressly the contrary [v. 14-26]. ... So that a reformation of life (included under repentance) was essential, & defects in this would be made up by their faith; i.e. their faith should be counted for righteousness [Romans 4:3, 5]. ... [A]dding a faith in God & His attributes that on their repentance He would pardon them [1 John 1:9], they also would be justified [Romans 3:24]. This then explains the text "there is no other name under heaven by which a man may be saved," [Acts

4:12] i.e., the defects in good works shall not be supplied by a faith in Mahomet, Foe, [i.e., Buddha], or any other except Christ.

What Barton is quoting from here are Jefferson's "Notes on Religion." These were notes made by Jefferson in 1776 in preparation for his arguments for the disestablishment of the Anglican Church in Virginia. It's quite clear from these notes that the two Locke works that Jefferson was using were his *Reasonableness of Christianity* and his *Letter on Toleration*. Barton is quoting from the part where Jefferson was using *Reasonableness of Christianity*.

What Barton quotes here wasn't some sort of statement of faith from Jefferson, or even from Locke. This part of Jefferson's notes was on a section of Locke's *Reasonableness of Christianity* where Locke was stating what Christians believed; where in the Bible those beliefs came from; and where the Bible as well as different "systems" of Christianity contradicted each other. It was essentially a comparison of what the Bible actually said and what people claimed it said. Remember, *Reasonableness of Christianity* was the work that got Locke branded a Socinian by theologian John Edwards and other prominent clergymen of his day.

The reason Jefferson would have found this particular part of Locke's *Reasonableness of Christianity* relevant in preparing his arguments for the disestablishment of the church was all the stuff Locke wrote in it about whether or not the Bible said that Gentiles, who had never heard the law of Moses or heard of Jesus, could still be "righteous" if they followed the law (which in their case would be the law of nature, derived from their own reason). But Barton chops out all references indicating what Locke's actual point was.

Barton doesn't even mention that what he's quoting is from Jefferson's "Notes on Religion," let alone the reason that Jefferson was making these notes. Instead, he describes what he quotes as Jefferson's "own personal summation of Locke's view of Christianity," which he claims "clearly shows that [Jefferson] definitely did not consider Locke to be a deist." Barton also heavily edits the quote. For example, he chops out (where his third ellipsis is), the words "all make the fundamental pillars of X^ty to be faith & repentance." Obviously, parts like this had to be cut out because words like "*all* make" show that this was a comparison of differing systems of Christianity, and not the statement of faith that Barton wants it to look like.

Here's what Jefferson actually wrote, without Barton's omissions (bolded here) and his additions of bracketed Bible verse references and other changes:

Locke's system of Christianity is this: Adam was created happy & immortal; **but his happiness was to have been** *Earthly & Earthly* **immortality.** By *sin* he lost this – so that he became subject to total death (like that of brutes) to the crosses & unhappiness of this life. At the intercession however of the son of god this sentence was in part remitted. **A life conformable to the law was to restore them again to immortality.** And moreover to them who *believed* their *faith* was to be counted for righteousness. Not that faith without works was to save them; St. James. c. 2. sais expressly the contrary; **& all make the fundamental pillars of X^ty to be faith &** *repentance.* So that a reformation of life (included under *repentance*) was essential, & defects in this would be made up by their *faith;* i.e. their faith should be counted for righteousness. **As to that part of mankind who never had the gospel preached to them, they are 1. Jews. – 2. Pagans, or Gentiles. The Jews had the law of works revealed to them. By this therefore they were to be saved: & a lively faith in god's promises to send the Messiah would supply small defects. 2. The Gentiles. St. Pa. sais – Rom. 2. 13. 'the Gentiles have the law written in their hearts, i.e. the law of nature: to which** adding a *faith* in God's & his attributes that on their repentance he would pardon them, they also would be justified. This then explains the text 'there is no other *name* under heaven by which a man may be saved,' i.e. the defects in good works shall not be supplied by a faith in Mahomet Foe, [?] or any other except Christ.[26]

26. Paul Leicester Ford, ed., *The Works of Thomas Jefferson,* vol. 2, (New York: G.P. Putnam's Sons, 1904), 253-254.

Since these were just notes, the best way to understand what Jefferson was talking about is to pull out a copy of Locke's *Reasonableness of Christianity* and follow Jefferson's notes while reading what he was making notes on. But since Barton doesn't even tell his readers what he's quoting that might be kind of tough for them to do. But, of course, the last thing that Barton wants his readers to do is to get some crazy idea like actually going and reading Jefferson's "Notes on Religion." If they did that they might read this last paragraph of those notes and see that Jefferson wasn't just talking about equality for the different denominations of Christians, as the revisionists are so fond of claiming.

> He [Locke] sais 'neither Pagan nor Mahomedan nor Jew ought to be excluded from the civil rights of the Commonwealth because of his religion.' Shall we suffer a Pagan to deal with us and not suffer him to pray to his god? Why have Xns. been distinguished above all people who have ever lived, for persecutions? Is it because it is the genius of their religion? No, it's genius is the reverse. It is the refusing toleration to those of a different opn which has produced all the bustles and wars on account of religion. It was the misfortune of mankind that during the darker centuries the Xn. priests following their ambition and avarice combining with the magistrate to divide the spoils of the people, could establish the notion that schismatics might be ousted of their possessions & destroyed. This notion we have not yet cleared ourselves from. In this case no wonder the oppressed should rebel, & they will continue to rebel & raise disturbance until their civil rights are fully restored to them & all partial distinctions, exclusions & incapacitations removed.[27]

27. Paul Leicester Ford, ed., *The Works of Thomas Jefferson*, vol. 2, (New York: G.P. Putnam's Sons, 1904), 267-268.

Barton's Lies About
Jefferson's Educational Endeavors
Prior to the University of Virginia

Barton doesn't immediately get to the University of Virginia after his section on Jefferson's own education, but segues into it with a section on the other various schools and education plans that Jefferson was involved with prior to his founding of the university, beginning this section with the following opening statement:

So, to the question of whether Jefferson rejected his own personal educational experience because it had been so thoroughly infused with religion, the answer is a clear "No!" Jefferson was involved with many educational endeavors throughout his life, and he consistently took deliberate actions to include religious instruction in each.

Now, we've already seen that Jefferson's own education was not "thoroughly infused with religion" – his boyhood teachers don't seem to have been any sort of religious influence on him at all; he wasn't taught Barton's religified version of the Scottish Common Sense philosophy; the professor he latched onto at William and Mary was the one non-clergyman there; he wasn't taught from the very religious Blackstone's *Commentaries* as a law student; and he did not reject the secular Enlightenment writers. This, of course, makes Barton's "logic" that Jefferson wouldn't have rejected his own religious education in his later educational plans and projects completely baseless to begin with.

As we'll see, every single example that Barton conjures up in his attempt to show that Jefferson "took deliberate actions to include religious instruction in each" of his educational endeavors is a lie.

The One About
Jefferson and John Witherspoon

BARTON'S LIE: Jefferson writing to Princeton president Rev. John Witherspoon when looking for teachers shows that Jefferson was trying to start religious schools.

THE TRUTH: John Witherspoon was one of several people Jefferson went to when looking for teachers for two schools in Virginia because Witherspoon, as the president of a college, was likely to know of recent graduates or other qualified individuals who were looking for teaching positions.

Here's how Barton presents the two instances of Jefferson writing to John Witherspoon when looking for teachers:

> For example, when a grammar school was being established in Jefferson's area in 1783, he wrote to the Rev. Dr. John Witherspoon, the head of Princeton (a university that trained Presbyterians for Gospel ministry), to request one of Witherspoon's students as an instructor for the school.

> In 1792, Jefferson again wrote the Reverend Witherspoon about another local school "in hopes that your seminary ... may furnish some person whom you could recommend"

to be the assistant to "the head of a school of considerable reputation in Virginia."

What would Jefferson expect from students trained by the Reverend Dr. Witherspoon? Certainly not a secular approach to education.

So, when asked on two occasions by friends in Virginia to help them find qualified teachers for their schools, Jefferson asked the president of a college if he knew of anyone he could recommend.

First of all, John Witherspoon wasn't the only person Jefferson contacted when looking for these teachers, and since the others he contacted about these same teaching positions had no particular connection to religion, he obviously didn't contact Witherspoon because he was seeking out someone who was religious. He wasn't even particularly looking for someone who had been trained by Witherspoon when he asked Witherspoon for recommendations.

Here's what Jefferson wrote in 1783 to Wilson Cary Nicholas, the friend who had asked him to help find a teacher for a school in Jefferson's home county in Virginia:

> I enquired at Princeton of Dr. Witherspoon. But he informed me that college was but just getting together again,[28] and that no such person could of course be had there. I enquired in Philadelphia for some literary character of the Irish nation in that city.[29]

And here's what Jefferson wrote to Witherspoon in 1792 when looking for a teaching assistant for another school in Virginia:

> The head of a school of considerable reputation in Virginia having

---

28. In June 1783, the Continental Congress had been forced to evacuate Philadelphia when about four hundred armed Continental Army soldiers stationed in Philadelphia surrounded Independence Hall demanding their back pay, and more soldiers from elsewhere in Pennsylvania were on their way to join those who were already there. The Congress moved to Princeton's Nassau Hall, the college's only building at the time, and remained there until November.

29. Thomas Jefferson to Wilson Cary Nicholas, December 31, 1783. Julian P. Boyd, ed., *The Papers of Thomas Jefferson,* vol. 6, (Princeton, NJ: Princeton University Press, 1952), 432.

occasion for an Assistant, I take the liberty of inclosing to you the letters I have received on that subject in hopes that your seminary, or your acquaintance may furnish some person, whom you could recommend as fitted to the object.[30]

In quoting this letter to Witherspoon, Barton just chops off the part of Jefferson's sentence that said "or your acquaintance may furnish some person," making it appear that Jefferson was specifically looking for someone from Princeton, and therefore, according to Barton, someone who was trained "for Gospel ministry." In both cases, Jefferson was just looking a qualified teacher, and Witherspoon, being the president of Princeton, was a likely person to know of a qualified teacher who was looking for a job.

In answer to Barton's question, "What would Jefferson expect from students trained by the Reverend Dr. Witherspoon?," well, he'd expect someone who was well educated in any number of subjects and certainly qualified to teach children. One of the big changes Witherspoon made as president of Princeton was to shift the college away from being predominantly a school to train ministers, greatly increasing the teaching of the sciences and other subjects. In fact, because of Witherspoon's changes, the school got so far away from being a theological seminary that in 1812 Princeton Theological Seminary was established as a separate school.

Jefferson was clearly aware that Princeton wasn't only a theological school. In January 1792, just two months before writing to Witherspoon looking for a teacher for the school in Virginia, Jefferson wrote the following letter of introduction to Witherspoon for a friend's son who was headed to Princeton, specifying which subjects that student was to study there – mathematics, natural philosophy (meaning science), and rhetoric.

The bearer hereof, Mr. Bennet Taylor, a young gentleman from Virginia, goes on to your seminary for the prosecution of his studies.

30. Thomas Jefferson to John Witherspoon, March 12, 1792. Charles T. Cullen, ed., *The Papers of Thomas Jefferson*, vol. 23, (Princeton, NJ: Princeton University Press, 1990), 271.

Being recommended to me by a good friend of mine, I feel an interest in his success, and therefore take the liberty of naming him particularly to you. His principal objects will be mathematics and Natural philosophy. Rhetoric also, I presume is taught with you, and will be proper for him as destined for the bar. As he has no time to spare, I have mentioned to him that I thought he might undertake the subject of Moral philosophy in his chamber, at leisure hours, and from books, without attending lectures or exercises in that branch.[31]

Apparently, Jefferson didn't even find it important for his friend's son to attend Witherspoon's lectures on moral philosophy, even though by this time Witherspoon actually *had* incorporated that Scottish Common Sense philosophy into them.

31. Thomas Jefferson to John Witherspoon, January 12, 1792. Charles T. Cullen, ed., *The Papers of Thomas Jefferson*, vol. 23, (Princeton, NJ: Princeton University Press, 1990), 40.

The One About
Jefferson and the Geneva Academy

BARTON'S LIE: In 1794, Jefferson wanted to bring a famous religious school from Europe to America.

THE TRUTH: The Geneva Academy, although originally founded by John Calvin in the 1500s as a theological seminary, was no longer a religious school in 1794. By that time it had been transformed into an academy of science. What Jefferson wanted to import was a group of Europe's top science professors, not a religious school.

According to Barton:

In 1794, after Jefferson had returned home from serving as secretary of state for President George Washington, he contacted a member of the Virginia legislature about bringing the Geneva Academy from Europe to Virginia. The Geneva Academy was established in 1559 by Reformation theologian John Calvin. In this school, the Bible was an indispensable textbook and students from the school became missionaries all over Europe; and Jefferson wanted to bring this famous religious school to his state.

Yes, the Geneva Academy was originally founded by John Calvin in 1559 as a theological seminary, but it wasn't a theological seminary in 1794 when Jefferson proposed moving it to America. By 1794 it had been transformed into one of the two best academies of science in Europe. Jefferson's plan was to import a group of Europe's top science professors, not a religious school.

In 1794, François D'Ivernois, an economist and political writer from Geneva, wrote to Thomas Jefferson and John Adams. Political upheaval in Geneva in the wake of the French Revolution had forced D'Ivernois into exile in England, and was threatening the future of the Geneva Academy. D'Ivernois, who had met both Jefferson and Adams in the 1780s when they were foreign ministers in Europe, wrote separately to each of them proposing that the faculty of the academy be relocated to the United States.

In a letter to George Washington, who was also anxious to establish a public university in America, Jefferson described the Geneva Academy and its faculty, listing the various sciences taught by the faculty members who D'Ivernois thought would be willing to move to America.

> ... the revolution which has taken place at Geneva has demolished the college of that place, which was in a great measure supported by the former government. The colleges of Geneva & Edinburgh were considered as the two eyes of Europe in matters of science, insomuch that no other pretended to any rivalship with either. Edinburgh has been the most famous in medicine during the life of Cullen; but Geneva most so in the other branches of science, and much the most resorted to from the continent of Europe because the French language was that which was used. a M^r. D'Ivernois, a Genevan, & man of science, known as the author of a history of that republic, has proposed the transplanting that college in a body to America. he has written to me on the subject, as he has also done to Mr. Adams, as he was formerly known to us both, giving us the details of his views for effecting it. probably these have been communicated to you by Mr. Adams, as D'Ivernois desired should be done; but lest they should not have been communicated I will take the liberty of doing it. his plan I think would

go to about ten or twelve professorships. he names to me the following professors as likely if not certain to embrace the plan.

Monchon, the present President, who wrote the Analytical table for the Encyclopedists, & which sufficiently proves his comprehensive science.

Pictet, known from his admeasurements of a degree, & other works, professor of Natural philosophy.

his brother, said by M. D'Ivernois to be also great.

Senebier, author of commentaries on Spallanzani, & of other works in Natural philosophy & Meteorology; also the translator of the Greek tragedies.

Bertrand ⎫ both mathematicians, and said to be inferior to
L'Huillier ⎭ nobody in that line except La Grange, who is without an equal.

Prevost, highly spoken of by D'Ivernois.

De Saussure & his son, formerly a professor, but who left the college to have more leisure to pursue his geological researches into the Alps, by which work he is very advantageously known.[32]

Does that sound like a religious school? Of course not. But it's an easy one for Barton to claim was a religious school because it had been at one time.

Barton's lie about this school is also a good example of his tricky footnoting. His paragraph about Jefferson's wanting to bring this school to America contains two footnotes. But, if you look at where in his paragraph his footnotes are, and go look up these footnotes (they're actually endnotes, so you don't even see them unless you flip to the back of the book), you'll see that they have absolutely nothing to do with the claim he's making about Jefferson. One of his footnotes is at the end of the sentence where he

32. Thomas Jefferson to George Washington, February 23, 1795. *The Thomas Jefferson Papers, Series 1, General Correspondence, 1651-1827,* Library of Congress Manuscript Division.

says that John Calvin founded the Geneva Academy in 1559, and the other is where he says that students from this school became missionaries. The source Barton cites in these two footnotes is a biography of John Calvin. But where *isn't* there a footnote? At the end of the last sentence, where he claims that Jefferson wanted to import a religious school to America. So Barton, by throwing in two footnotes for facts that are completely unnecessary to document, gives his readers the impression that his claim about Jefferson is documented while not actually documenting this claim at all.

The One About
Jefferson and Gideon Blackburn's Indian School

BARTON'S LIE: In 1803, President Jefferson gave federal money to an Indian mission school opened by Rev. Gideon Blackburn to pay for religious instruction among the Cherokees.

THE TRUTH: Gideon Blackburn's plan was to *not* try to teach religion to the Cherokees, at least not right away. Blackburn thought the failure of other missionaries was because they tried to convert the Indians to Christianity first, before trying to educate and "civilize" them. Blackburn wanted to try the reverse – "civilizing" the Cherokees by first turning them into farmers and educating their children *before* trying to convert them to Christianity. Jefferson approved a small amount of money for supplies for Blackburn's school, whose primary purpose in 1803, and for the foreseeable future, was going to be instructing the Cherokees in agriculture.

According to Barton:

In 1803, while serving as president, Jefferson met with Presbyterian minister Gideon Blackburn at the White House about opening a missionary school for Cherokees near Knoxville, Tennessee. The school was to include religious instruction as a primary part of its studies, and President

Jefferson directed Secretary of War Henry Dearborn to give federal money to help the school achieve its objectives.

A big goal of the federal government in the early 1800s was to get the Indians to shift from being hunter-gathers to being farmers. The idea was that getting Indians to settle on farms and stay in one place would increase the safety of white settlers. To make this happen, the government supported any plan for agricultural education among the Indians. This meant supporting Indian mission schools, since they were the only game in town.

As I wrote about in *Liars For Jesus,* one big example of how the government tried to advance its turning-the-Indians-into-farmers strategy was a bill passed by Congress in 1819, which provided for small government grants to be given annually to any school that included agricultural education in its curriculum. The Indian schools that received these grants were, of course, virtually all run by missionaries, but it was specified that the government funding was to "instruct them in the mode of agriculture suited to their situation,"[33] not for religious education.

A big part of this plan was to make the cost to the government minimal by increasing private donations to the Indian schools. The reasoning was that if people saw that the government was giving money to Indian schools, it would increase public confidence that the idea of "civilizing" the Indians wasn't a lost cause (which was how most people had begun to see it), and make it easier for the Indian schools to raise money through private donations. This actually worked, since this was a time when the American people assumed that if the government was funding something, it couldn't be a crazy idea. The government grants to these Indian schools were very small, most of them only about $50 (roughly $700 in today's money), but this small show of government backing resulted in a big increase in private donations. The result was that the public, rather than the government, was picking up most of the tab for

---

33. Richard Peters, ed., *The Public Statutes at Large of the United States of America,* vol. 3, (Boston: Charles C. Little and James Brown, 1846), 516-517.

something that the government wanted to make happen.

This appears to be exactly what Jefferson did in 1803 with Gideon Blackburn's school – a school whose primary purpose was going to be teaching agriculture to the Cherokees. He approved a small amount of funding, providing Blackburn with an official recommendation of the school from the president to show potential private donors for his fundraising.

This is one of those weird cases where what would normally be the best primary source – what Gideon Blackburn himself wrote – is probably the most unreliable source of all. The reason for this is that in almost every letter and everything else he wrote about his school Blackburn was constantly fundraising, either trying to get more donations from private citizens or more funding from the Presbyterian Church. Because of this motive of fundraising, Blackburn exaggerated about everything. Therefore, it's necessary to do the unusual thing of using secondary sources to fact check the primary source.

The various accounts I've been able to find regarding what, exactly, the funding approved for Gideon Blackburn's school in 1803 was are a bit sketchy and differ on some points, but they all pretty much agree on the basics. The amount of the funding approved by Jefferson was a few hundred dollars (the amount varies in the different accounts from $200 to a little over $400). It is not clear whether this funding was to recur annually or if it was a one shot deal. The funding approved by Jefferson was taken out of the funds already appropriated for the Cherokee Indian Agency. The government's Indian agent to the Cherokees, Col. Return J. Meigs, purchased blankets and hired carpenters to build a dormitory for the students, presumably using the funding approved by Jefferson for the school.

Whatever the details, the one thing that's important here is clear – the funding for this school was approved by Jefferson because the school was going to be teaching the Cherokees to farm. It was not, as Barton claims, because the "school was to include religious instruction as a primary part of its studies." Even the Presbyterian General Assembly, while of course hoping to convert

Indians to Christianity while teaching them to be more like white people, didn't include religious instruction when describing the purpose of the school:

> Mr. Blackburn is taking measures, under the auspices of the committee of missions, for establishing a school on the borders of the Indian Territory, for the purpose of instructing the Indian youth in the English language, Agriculture and the mechanical arts, and other branches of useful knowledge.[34]

If it seems weird that the Presbyterian Church not only didn't make religion the primary purpose of this school, but didn't even mention religion at all in its purpose, there actually was a reason for this in the case of this particular school. In order to get the Cherokee chiefs to allow him to open his school, Blackburn had to promise them that he *wouldn't* be teaching religion.

The reason the Cherokees approved Blackburn's school was because they wanted to replace the Moravian missionaries who they had reluctantly given permission, on a three-year trial basis, to open a school in 1799. At the end of the three years, the Cherokees decided to give the Moravians the boot because all they had been doing was preaching and trying to convert them. They hadn't even gotten around to actually building the school they promised. So, when the Cherokees agreed in 1803 to let Blackburn open his school, it was on a two year trial basis and on the condition that he wouldn't be preaching or teaching religion.

Blackburn may have just been trying to make lemons into lemonade, but he actually does seem to have genuinely thought at the time he made this promise that not being able to teach religion to the Cherokees might be a good thing. Blackburn came up with the idea that the reason Indian missions always failed miserably at converting any Indians to Christianity might be because the missionaries, like the Moravians that he was replacing, tried to convert

---

34. *Extracts from the Minutes of the General Assembly of the Presbyterian Church in the United States of America; A.D. 1803,* (Philadelphia: Jane Aitken, 1803), 15.

the Indians to Christianity first, before trying to educate them in other subjects and teach them to farm. Blackburn was going to try the reverse – turning the Cherokees into farmers and educating their children first, and not trying to convert them to Christianity until *after* they were educated and "civilized," when they might be more open to learning about Christianity.

Once his school was open, however, Blackburn apparently forgot all about his novel idea and also ignored the promise he had made not to teach religion, causing almost all of the full-blooded Cherokees to pull their children out of his school, leaving him with only the mixed-blood children, whose white fathers wanted so badly for their children to have an English education that they were willing to keep sending them to Blackburn's school.

Blackburn then made himself even more unpopular when he started sticking his nose into the Cherokees' politics, pushing the mixed-blood Cherokees to impose Christianity on their people by law by advocating for marriage laws, laws against birth control, Sabbath laws, etc.

But it was Blackburn's whiskey run in 1809 that would completely end what was left of his relationship with the Cherokees.

In addition to being an Indian missionary and pastor of his own white congregation in Tennessee, Blackburn was in the whiskey business, operating a distillery with his brother not far from his Indian school. He also had his eye on a piece of land in the Cherokee territory that he wanted for himself. In 1809, he saw an opportunity to both sell some whiskey and possibly get the government to help him get the land he wanted.

Blackburn had heard from his War Department friends that the government wanted to explore the waterways between Tennessee and the Gulf of Mexico, so he volunteered for the job, proposing the idea that a boat carrying whiskey from his distillery would be a good cover for a secret expedition to explore the waterways. The government went for the idea. Blackburn and his brother loaded a barge with over two thousand gallons of whiskey, and told everyone it was just a business venture to sell whiskey in Mobile, Alabama. Things went very wrong, however, when Blackburn's barge was stopped as it entered Creek territory, where his whiskey was confiscated by the Creek chief.[35]

Although Blackburn wasn't doing anything illegal in transporting whiskey, since it was supposedly intended for white customers and not Indians, his crew had been trading and selling it to Indians along the way, in violation of federal law. Because of this, it was suspected that the reason Blackburn had put a half-blood Cherokee (a former student of his school) in charge of the crew was to evade the law. It wasn't illegal for one Indian to sell or trade whiskey to other Indians. It was only illegal for whites to do it.

To make a long story short, the confiscation of Blackburn's whiskey by the Creeks led to his secret government mission being exposed, and that was the end of Blackburn's relationship with the Cherokees. Neither the Creeks nor the Cherokees, including the mixed-blood Cherokees, wanted white merchants using their lands to transport whiskey or anything else. This was already a hot button issue between the Indians and the government at the time this happened. Once the truth about Blackburn's whiskey trip was revealed, even the mixed-blood Cherokees pulled their children out of his schools (he had two schools by this time), and the schools were closed.

Barton's version of the Gideon Blackburn story, while in no way being an example of Jefferson's promoting religion, is a great example of something else – just how far Barton actually goes with his deceptive footnoting.

Barton lists three different sources in his endnote for his Blackburn story. One is the entry for Gideon Blackburn in the 1929 *Dictionary of American Biography.* Another is a 1974 article about Blackburn in a Presbyterian history journal. Neither of these is a primary source, but at least they are sources that actually exist.

Barton's third source, on the other hand, which does appear to

---

35. Other details of these events, which include Blackburn involving Cherokees who had attended his mission school in transporting his whiskey, are outside the scope of this book. An 1810 letter from the attorney general of Tennessee to James Madison tells much more of the story, but since this book is specifically about Thomas Jefferson, I'm not going to get into the part of the story that carried over into the Madison administration here.

be a primary source, is completely bogus. What Barton gives is a page number in the *Debates and Proceedings* of the 7th Congress.

Since Barton only says that this Blackburn thing happened in 1803, and the 7th Congress ended in 1803, this footnote would appear to be legitimate to any of his readers who might happen to glance at his sources. But the 7th Congress ended in *March* of 1803. The 1803 Presbyterian General Assembly that appointed Blackburn as a missionary to the Cherokees in the first place didn't take place until the middle of May, and Blackburn didn't get his school approved by the Cherokees until October, after returning to Tennessee sometime before September. This means that Blackburn must have gone to Jefferson for funding sometime between the end of May and September, months after the 7th Congress ended. So, obviously, Barton's footnote can't be right.

Now, Barton's footnotes quite often don't support his claims. That's expected. But at least they usually have *something* to do with whatever he's babbling about. Not in this case. If you look up the page that Barton cites expecting to find some congressional record that's at least *somehow* related to an Indian school or the Cherokees or even Tennessee, you won't. What's on the page he cites is a completely unrelated act of Congress. But it's not just any completely unrelated act of Congress. It's an act of Congress that he lies about elsewhere in his book. It's as if he just picked something from another of his endnotes that was from the right year and looked *congressional* and stuck it in the endnote for his Blackburn story! Seriously, you just can't make this crap up.

The One About
Jefferson and the Ursuline Nuns

BARTON'S LIE: Jefferson promised some sort of unspecified federal aid to a Catholic school in New Orleans in 1804.

THE TRUTH: Jefferson replied to a letter from the nuns who ran this school to allay their concerns about the status of their convent's property after the Louisiana Purchase.

When the United States purchased the Louisiana Territory from France in 1803 (1804 in Barton's book), the nuns at the Ursuline convent in New Orleans, like many of the territory's inhabitants, were concerned about the status of their property. The Ursulines' convent and school had been built on land granted by the government of France in 1734, and much of the income that supported these institutions came from two other properties, granted by the later Spanish government. Following the purchase of the territory, a wide variety of rumors was spread by anti-American natives of New Orleans. Among these were two about the convent. One was that the United States government planned to confiscate the convent's property and immediately expel the nuns from the country. The other was that no new novices would be allowed to enter the convent, but that the government would let the nuns who were already there stay, and then take the property after they all died off.

Several other events that took place in New Orleans increased the nuns' concerns. One of these was the closing of another Catholic church by U.S. officials who were trying to stop a dispute between the followers of two rival priests from becoming violent. Because of this particular event, the nuns wrote to Jefferson requesting to have their property officially confirmed to them by Congress. Jefferson wrote back assuring them that their property was secure, and that they had nothing to fear from the United States government because their school would have "all the protection [his] office [could] give it."[36] But, because Jefferson also used the word "patronage" in his letter to the nuns, Barton, by italicizing the word patronage in his quote from the letter and adding the word "support" in brackets next to it, implies that Jefferson granted some sort of federal aid to this religious school.

All that Jefferson meant when he said in his letter that the work of the nuns' school "cannot fail to ensure it the patronage of the government it is under" was that the U.S. officials who had shut down the church to stop the fight over the rival priests would never have any reason to do anything like that to a school. The words "the government it is under" were actually referring to the local government officials in New Orleans, not the federal government. By the "protection of [his] office," Jefferson (who already thought that the local U.S. officials in New Orleans had overstepped their authority by interfering in a church dispute) was assuring the nuns that the local U.S. officials were under the control of his office and would be stopped in the unlikely event that they ever did try to interfere with the convent's school.

This Ursuline nuns story is a perfect example of how Barton can take a single word from a letter, and, by ripping it from both its textual and historical context, can so easily turn it into a lie about Jefferson aiding religion.

---

36. Thomas Jefferson to Sr. Therese de St. Xavier Farjon, July 13 or 14, 1804. *The Thomas Jefferson Papers Series 1, General Correspondence, 1651-1827*, Library of Congress Manuscript Division.

The One About
Jefferson and Public School Bible Reading

BARTON'S LIE: Jefferson authored a plan of education for the public schools of Washington D.C. that included Bible reading.

THE TRUTH: Jefferson was elected president of the Washington D.C. school board in 1805 when he was president of the United States, but he had nothing to do with authoring the plan of education for the city's schools. The school that used the Bible as a reading text didn't even open until 1812, three years after Jefferson had left the presidencies of both the United States and the school board.

According to Barton:

> ... as a trustee, Jefferson did contribute much to the new school system and is credited with being "the chief author of the first plan of public education adopted for the city of Washington." When the first report of the Washington public schools was released to demonstrate the progress of the students in the new schools, it noted:

> > Fifty-five have learned to read in the Old and New Testaments, and are all able to spell words of three, four, and five syllables; twenty-six are now learning

> to read Dr. Watts' *Hymns* and spell words of two
> syllables; ten are learning words of four and five
> letters. Of fifty-nine out of the whole number
> admitted that did not know a single letter, twenty
> can now read the Bible and spell words of three,
> four, and five syllables; twenty-nine read Dr Watts'
> *Hymns* and spell words of two syllables, and ten,
> words of four and five letters.

This lie is constructed by taking the fact that in 1805, while serving as president, Jefferson was named as president of the brand new Washington D.C. school board, and then combining that fact with a report from a school in Washington D.C. that said the school was using the Bible as a reading text. The problem with this story? The school that the report was from didn't even open until three years after Jefferson had left Washington.

Barton does two things here. First he exaggerates Jefferson's involvement in the Washington D.C. schools, making him the author of the curriculum. Then he omits the dates that would show that the report he quotes is from a school that didn't even exist yet when Jefferson was president of the school board. The result, of course, is that Barton's readers will think that Jefferson authored a curriculum for public schools that included Bible reading.

In reality, Jefferson had almost nothing to do with the founding of Washington D.C.'s public schools. He made a sizeable donation of $200 when money was being raised to start the school system, and he was elected president of the school board at an 1805 meeting (which he didn't even attend), but he never took an active role as president of the school board. The only other mention of Jefferson anywhere in the minutes of the school board besides his being elected its president had to do with his securing the land grant for the lot in Washington that one of the first two schools would be built on. But even that was in his capacity as President of the United States, not president of the school board.

Jefferson had nothing whatsoever to do with the curriculum for the schools in Washington. Barton's claim that he was credited with being "the chief author of the first plan of public education adopted for the city of Washington" is a misrepresentation of what was written in an article in an 1895 issue of the *Records of the Columbia Historical Society*, the source cited by Barton in his endnotes.

First of all, the article's statement about Jefferson being the "author" of the plan wasn't even referring to the curriculum. It was referring to the plan of how the school system would be run, (i.e., the number of schools, that students who could pay would be required to pay tuition, but poor students would attend for free, etc.). Because many aspects of the plan for Washington's schools were similar to what Jefferson had proposed decades earlier in his plan for public schools in Virginia, the author of the article wrote:

Mr Jefferson's early and liberal contribution in money and his accepting and holding the offices of trustee and president of the board of trustees of public schools so long as he resided here show his personal interest in their establishment, and the fact that he had several years earlier proposed a quite similar plan of education for the state of Virginia and a few years later, in 1817, vigorously renewed his proposal, make a strong probability that he himself was the chief author of the first plan of public education adopted for the city of Washington.[37]

Barton then follows his out-of-context quote from this article with what he describes as "the first report of the Washington public schools," quoting a part of this report about the Bible being used as a reading textbook.

First of all, this report wasn't a report on *schools* plural; it was a report from one specific school – the Lancasterian school that opened in 1812.

Between the years of 1806 and 1811, the Washington City school board attempted to establish and maintain two public schools in

37. *Records of the Columbia Historical Society*, vol. 1, (Washington D.C.: Columbia Historical Society, 1895), 122-123.

the city. The board's biggest problem was that they couldn't afford to pay high enough salaries to get and keep qualified teachers. Classes were held in rented buildings until enough money was raised through private donations to build two schoolhouses in 1807. By 1809, the City Council had cut the public funding for these schools nearly in half, and one of the two was closed. These first two schools were the only schools that existed at the time that Jefferson was president of the school board.

In 1811, the teacher of a Lancasterian school in Georgetown wrote a letter to the Washington City school board suggesting that they might have more success with this type of school. Lancasterian schools were developed by Joseph Lancaster in England as an economical way to educate large numbers of poor children. By using the older students to teach the younger ones, Lancaster's system allowed one teacher to oversee the education of hundreds of children. The school in Georgetown was teaching three hundred and fifty students with one teacher.

In 1812, the Washington City school board decided to try the Lancasterian method. Henry Ould, a teacher trained by Joseph Lancaster in England, was brought over to run the new Lancasterian school. Even without the fact that this school didn't open until three years after Jefferson left Washington, just the fact that this school was a Lancasterian school disproves Barton's claim that Thomas Jefferson authored the school's plan of education. A Lancasterian school was called a Lancasterian school because it used the educational plan developed by Joseph Lancaster.

The date that this school opened, the fact that it was a Lancasterian school, and a thorough explanation of what a Lancasterian school was is all found in one of the sources that Barton himself cites in his endnotes – an 1875 book titled *History of the Public Schools of Washington City, D.C., from August, 1805, to August, 1875*. Did Barton just not read this book that he himself cites, or is he deliberately ignoring what it says so he can tell his lies? Yeah, I'm going with the latter.

We are now at the end of Barton's section on Jefferson's pre-University of Virginia educational endeavors, so let's stop for a quick recap. Here's a list of the *true* stories that Barton distorted in this section to create what he claims are examples of Jefferson taking "deliberate actions to include religious instruction in" education.

1. On two occasions, Jefferson contacted Princeton president John Witherspoon to see if he knew of anyone he could recommend for teaching positions at schools in Virginia.

2. In 1794, Jefferson wanted to bring a group of Europe's top science professors from the Geneva Academy to America.

3. In 1803, Jefferson approved a small amount of funding for an Indian mission school whose main purpose at that time was going to be teaching agriculture.

4. In 1804, Jefferson wrote a letter to some nuns in New Orleans to assure them that their convent's property was safe after the Louisiana Purchase.

5. In 1813, a school in Washington D.C. that Jefferson had absolutely nothing to do was using the Bible as a reading textbook.

But, based on *his* versions of these stories, Barton segues into his section on the University of Virginia with this:

In short, Jefferson was involved with many educational endeavors prior to establishing the University of Virginia in 1819, and in none of them was there any attempt to exclude religious instruction. To the contrary – in each case he took intentional steps to include or preserve it. So with this background, what about the four oft-repeated claims about Jefferson excluding religion from the university he founded?

Now, for some reason, Barton's four "oft-repeated claims" about the University of Virginia that he listed at the beginning of his chapter as the questions he was going to answer (see page 1) are a bit different from the questions he uses as his section headings for the rest of his chapter, so we'll just go with the questions he asks now, which are:

1. Was the University of Virginia Founded as a Secular University?

2. Was Jefferson's Faculty Composed of Unitarians?

3. Did Jefferson Bar Religious Instruction from the Academic Program?

4. Did the University of Virginia Have Chaplains?

1. Was the University of Virginia Founded as a Secular University?

Barton begins this section by pointing out that universities in colonial America were founded by specific religious denominations. He then asserts that the University of Virginia was different – not because Jefferson founded it as a secular university, but because he founded it as a "transdenominational" university. He then sets out to prove this assertion with a whole bunch of stuff that just isn't true.

The One About
Jefferson and Rev. Samuel Knox

BARTON'S LIE: Jefferson used a plan from a 1799 paper written by Presbyterian minister Rev. Samuel Knox, "implementing" Knox's plan to establish multiple theological schools at the University of Virginia and to form a "transdenominational" school. Jefferson also wanted Knox to be a professor at the university.

THE TRUTH: Jefferson did, in 1822, invite the different religious sects of Virginia to establish their own theological schools near the university, but this had nothing to do with the (very different) plan

73

proposed by Samuel Knox in 1799. Jefferson's invitation to the religious sects was nothing more than a way to stop the clergy's attacks on the university, and no theological schools were ever actually established. Additionally, Jefferson did not want Knox, or any other clergyman, as a professor at the university. Jefferson even went as far as lying to Knox to keep him away.

According to Barton:

In 1799 the Reverend Knox penned a policy paper proposing the formation of a state university that would invite many denominations to establish multiple theological schools rather than just one, so they would work together in mutual Christian cooperation rather than competition. Jefferson agreed with Knox's philosophy, and it was this model that he employed at his University of Virginia. (In fact, Jefferson invited the Reverend Knox to be the very *first* professor at the University, but because of a miscommunication, Knox did not respond to the offer in a timely fashion, so his teaching slot was finally offered to someone else.)

The miscommunication that Barton refers to occurred in 1817, when the board of Central College, the forerunner of the University of Virginia,[38] was wrongly informed that Samuel Knox had retired from teaching. At its July 1817 meeting, the Central College board voted to offer Knox its professorship of languages, but hearing that he had retired from teaching, rescinded this offer at its next meeting in October 1817. Jefferson was on this board, but he was only one vote out of six, and it is not known how he voted.

It is certainly clear, however, that Jefferson did not want Knox to be a professor at the University of Virginia. In fact, a year after

---

38. Central College was what the University of Virginia was called from 1816 to 1818. Central College, although started as a private institution with private donations, was intended from the start by Jefferson to become a state university. It never opened under the name Central College, but the university's construction was begun under that name.

the board of Central College voted to offer Knox a professorship, Jefferson lied to him to stop him from trying to get hired by the university.

A letter that Knox wrote to Jefferson in November 1818 indicates that Knox never even knew that the Central College board had planned to offer him a professorship in 1817. He had only just heard from a friend who had run into Jefferson's nephew, who was also on the Central College board, that there had been talk of his being offered a position.[39] So it wasn't that he didn't respond to Central College's offer in a timely fashion, as Barton says. The board had never gotten as far as sending him anything to respond to.

As it turned out, Knox had not retired from teaching, and he absolutely did want a professorship at the University of Virginia. He practically begged Jefferson for one when he wrote to him in 1818. Much of Knox's six page letter was essentially his résumé, with a direct request that the university hire him – a request that Jefferson clearly had no intention of granting.

Now, here's where it gets interesting. Jefferson's reply to Knox's 1818 letter was an obvious pack of lies, the biggest of which was telling Knox that he was only helping Central College get established by the legislature as the state university, and that once this was accomplished he would no longer be involved enough to make decisions regarding the faculty.

Here's the most obvious of the lies that Jefferson told Knox:

> As to myself, I give all the aid I can towards it into existence, but, that done, age, and declining health and strength will oblige me to leave to younger characters the details of execution.[40]

This was a complete load of bull. Jefferson had no intention of leaving *anything* to anyone else. He planned to be, and was, thoroughly involved in every single decision about the university until

---

39. Samuel Knox to Thomas Jefferson, November 30, 1818. *The Thomas Jefferson Papers, Series 1, General Correspondence, 1651-1827*, Library of Congress Manuscript Division.
40. Thomas Jefferson to Samuel Knox, December 11, 1818. Ibid.

the day he died. His health was just fine. This was the same year that he rode thirty miles on horseback through a blizzard to get to a university board meeting at James Madison's house, forcing a much younger board member who was about to stop and stay put because of the weather to keep going when he was told along the way that the seventy-five-year-old Jefferson had already passed by and had kept going. (As a number of his letters show, the older Jefferson, who by all accounts was extraordinarily healthy and active until the very last days of his life, had no problem playing the age card when he didn't want to do something.)

Jefferson also told Knox that the board couldn't act on any applications until the legislature officially named Central College the state university, even though it was quite clear from Knox's letter that he realized that any position there wouldn't be immediate and that he was perfectly willing to wait until they were ready to start hiring.

At the same Central College board meeting where it was decided to withdraw the offer to Knox based on the rumor that he had retired, the board agreed to hire Dr. Thomas Cooper (who we'll hear much more about) as the university's professor of law and chemistry. And, not only had they agreed to hire Cooper, but it was decided that Jefferson would ask Cooper to help them find a professor of languages. When Knox wrote to Jefferson a year later asking him for a professorship, the professorship of languages that Central College had already voted to offer him had not been filled, and Knox was clearly willing to wait until the university was approved by the legislature and was ready to start hiring its professors, and yet Jefferson blew him off. If Jefferson had voted in favor of Knox when the Central College board voted in 1817 to offer him the professorship of languages, why would he have blown him off when he found out that he was available and wanted this position that still hadn't been filled? What other conclusion can possibly be drawn from this than that Jefferson just did not want Knox as a professor?

And what about this plan for multiple theological schools that Barton claims Jefferson got from Knox? Well, Knox's 1799 plan for multiple theological schools was nothing at all like what Jefferson proposed in 1822, so Jefferson's proposal obviously didn't come from Knox's paper. Jefferson's plan wasn't about getting the various religious sects to "work together in mutual Christian cooperation." It was just a way to stop the attacks on the university by the clergy.

But, before getting into what Jefferson did at the University of Virginia in 1822, and the major differences between the 1799 plan proposed by Samuel Knox and what Jefferson proposed, there's another lie that Barton throws into this story at this point that we need to get out of the way.

The One About
Jefferson and the College of William and Mary

BARTON'S LIE: Jefferson didn't secularize the College of William and Mary when he was on the college's Board of Visitors in 1779. He took deliberate actions to promote Christianity there – just not specifically the Anglican version of Christianity. He also appointed a missionary from the college to promote Christianity to the Indians.

THE TRUTH: Jefferson did secularize the College of William and Mary when he was on the college's Board of Visitors in 1779. He abolished the college's divinity school and replaced all of the religious professors with professors of secular subjects. He did not appoint a missionary from the college to promote Christianity to the Indians. He transformed an existing religious mission to the Indians that he didn't have the authority to abolish completely into an anthropological mission to study the culture and languages of the Indians.

Barton's first lie in his section about the University of Virginia is actually a lie about what Jefferson did in 1779 at his alma mater, the College of William and Mary. Like everything else so far, this one is another part of his set up for his lies about the university. Barton's claim here is that secularists "erroneously point to what Jefferson did with his own alma mater's Professor of Divinity as another alleged 'proof' of his commitment to religion-free education."

According to Barton:

Jefferson abolished the school of Divinity because it was solely an arm of the state-established Anglican Church, and he wanted to open the college to greater involvement by those from other Christian denominations. Further evidence that his reorganization of the college was not secular was his stipulation that "[T]he said professors shall likewise appoint from time to time a missionary of approved veracity to the several tribes of Indians." Jefferson took steps to ensure that the gospel was promoted at William and Mary but not just according to the thirty-nine Anglican articles and that church's denominational catechism.

As you've probably already gathered, Barton's big claim about the University of Virginia (when he finally does get to the University of Virginia) is going to be that Jefferson was not trying to make his university a non-Christian school, but merely trying to make it a school for all Christian denominations – a *transdenominational* or *nonpreferential* school. Barton is using basically the same lie for his claim about what Jefferson did at William and Mary, claiming that the only problem Jefferson had with that college was that it was an institution of a particular denomination. The truth is that Jefferson really did get rid of religion at William and Mary. Nothing about what he did there was "to ensure that the gospel was promoted."

For his evidence that Jefferson promoted Christianity at William and Mary, Barton uses a quote about the college's Brafferton Indian school from Jefferson's bill to amend the college's constitution.

"[T]he said professors shall likewise appoint from time to time a missionary of approved veracity to the several tribes of Indians."

Jefferson did *not* advocate this mission to promote Christianity to the Indians. He was stuck with it because it was written into the original charter of the college. What Jefferson actually proposed in his bill to amend the college's constitution was to turn this Indian mission into an anthropological rather than a religious mission.

The Indian mission, called the Brafferton Professorship, had been established with a private donation from the will of English (or Irish, depending on who's trying to claim him) scientist Robert Boyle. The funding was provided by the rental of Brafferton, an estate in England purchased by the executors of Boyle's will. The 1693 charter of William and Mary had specified that the college was to train young Indian boys in the Anglican religion to become missionaries to their people. In 1697 the income from the Brafferton estate was earmarked for this purpose, and the position became known as the Brafferton Professorship.

The Indian school at the college was a failure from the start. The biggest problem was that the Indians didn't want to send their children to a white school. In fact, the school's first six students were actually boys who were purchased from enemy tribes that had captured them. Although the college's charter called for twenty Indian students at a time, in 1721 there were none at all. Nevertheless, the Brafferton building was built in 1723 as a permanent home for the school, which struggled along for the next fifty years. The last Indian student was admitted in 1775. There is no evidence that any student who attended this school ever became a Christian missionary.

Benjamin Franklin, who found the whole idea of sending Indian children to white schools ridiculous, wrote the following satirical account of one attempt to recruit students for the Brafferton School:

...Our laborious manner of Life compared with theirs, they esteem slavish and base; and the Learning on which we value ourselves; they regard as frivolous and useless. An Instance of this occurred at the Treaty of Lancaster in Pennsylvania, Anno 1744, between the Government of Virginia & the Six Nations. After the principal Business was settled, the Commissioners from Virginia acquainted the Indians by a Speech, that there was at Williams-burg a College with a Fund for Educating Indian Youth, and that if the Chiefs of the Six-Nations would send down half a dozen of their Sons to that College, the Government would take Care that they should be well provided for, and instructed in all the Learning of the white People. It is one of the Indian Rules of Politeness not to answer a public Proposition the same day that it is made; they think it would be treating it as a light Matter; and that they show it Respect by taking time to consider it, as of a Matter important. They therefore deferred their Answer till the day following; when their Speaker began by expressing their deep Sense of the Kindness of the Virginia Government, in making them that Offer; for we know, says he, that you highly esteem the kind of Learning taught in those Colleges, and that the Maintenance of our Young Men while with you, would be very expensive to you. We are convinced therefore that you mean to do us good by your Proposal, and we thank you heartily. But you who are wise must know, that different Nations have different Conceptions of things; and you will therefore not take it amiss, if our Ideas of this Kind of Education happen not to be the same with yours. We have had some Experience of it: Several of our Young People were formerly brought up at the Colleges of the Northern Provinces; they were instructed in all your Sciences; but when they came back to us, they were bad Runners, ignorant of every means of living in the Woods, unable to bear either Cold or Hunger, knew neither how to build a Cabin, take a Deer, or kill an Enemy, spoke our Language imperfectly; were therefore neither fit for Hunters, Warriors, or Counsellors; they were totally good for nothing. We are however not the less obliged by your kind Offer, tho we decline accepting it; and to show our grateful Sense of it, if the Gentlemen of Virginia will send us a dozen of their Sons, we will take great Care of their Education, instruct them in all we know, and make Men of them.[41]

In 1779, when Jefferson became governor of Virginia, he also became a member of William and Mary's Board of Visitors. He immediately set to work on reorganizing the college to try to turn it into a non-religious state university. The biggest problem Jefferson faced

---

41. J.A. Leo Lemay, ed., *Benjamin Franklin, Writings*, (New York: Literary Classics of the United States, 1987), 969-970.

was that the Board of Visitors did not have the authority to make any changes that required amending the college's constitution. These changes could only be made by the legislature.

Among the changes that the board could not make was to increase the college's number of professors. They could, however, change what each professor taught. William and Mary's constitution limited the number of professorships to five, plus the Brafferton. At the time that Jefferson joined the board, the college had a divinity school with two professors. There was also a professor of Latin and Greek. Jefferson got rid of all three of these and replaced them with professors of law and police (meaning political science, not law enforcement), anatomy and medicine, and modern languages. Jefferson's reason for abolishing the school of Latin and Greek, which he referred to as the "grammar" school, was unrelated to getting rid of the theology schools. He just thought that this school attracted students who were too young for college and were disruptive.

Unlike the other professorships, the Brafferton Professorship couldn't be changed into a professorship for an entirely different subject. It still had to be an Indian mission. So, Jefferson's idea was to take advantage of this mission to study the Indians' culture and languages. As he made very clear in his *Notes on the State of Virginia,* his intent was to turn this professorship into a non-religious position, but he couldn't officially eliminate instruction in Christianity as part of the position because it was required by its founder.

The purposes of the Brafferton institution would be better answered by maintaining a perpetual mission among the Indian tribes, the object of which, besides instructing them in the principles of Christianity, as the founder requires, should be to collect their traditions, laws, customs, languages, and other circumstances which might lead to a discovery of their relation with one another, or descent from other nations. When these objects are accomplished with one tribe, the missionary might pass on to another.[42]

42. Albert Ellery Bergh, ed., *The Writings of Thomas Jefferson*, vol. 2, (Washington D.C.: Thomas Jefferson Memorial Association, 1907), 210.

Jefferson's repurposing of the Brafferton professorship would not only provide an opportunity to learn about the Indians, but would remove the Indian school from the grounds of William and Mary, getting rid of the last remaining religious school at the college.

In his *Bill for Amending the Constitution of the College of William and Mary*, Jefferson specified what the duties of the Brafferton Professorship would be, renaming the position "Missionary for Indian History, etc." He also made it very clear that it was for these specified non-religious duties that the Brafferton Professor would be paid with college funds. This bill is what Barton plucks the quote he uses from. Barton just chops off the whole part of the sentence that says that the duties of this "missionary" for "Indian history, etc." were not going to be religious.

> The said Professors shall likewise appoint, from time to time, a missionary, of approved veracity, to the several tribes of Indians, whose business shall be to investigate their laws, customs, religions, traditions, and more particularly their languages, constructing grammars thereof, as well as may be, and copious vocabularies, and, on oath, to communicate, from time to time to the said president and professors the materials he collects to be by them laid up and preserved in their library, for which trouble the said missionary shall be allowed a salary at the discretion of the visitors out of the revenues of the college.[43]

The Brafferton Professorship is really the only thing that revisionists like Barton can find that can be twisted to make it appear that Jefferson was promoting Christianity at William and Mary, but, as you can see, even this piece of *evidence* doesn't hold up. Jefferson did, in fact, secularize William and Mary. He got rid of all religious instruction, replacing the theological professorships with professorships of entirely non-religious subjects, and proposed to turn the one religious professorship that he didn't have the power

---

43. Julian P. Boyd, ed., *The Papers of Thomas Jefferson*, vol. 2, (Princeton, NJ: Princeton University Press, 1950), 540.

to entirely abolish into a non-religious, anthropological "mission." But that doesn't stop Barton from claiming that the Brafferton Professorship is proof that "Jefferson took steps to ensure that the gospel was promoted at William and Mary."

The One About
Jefferson Establishing Theological Seminaries

BARTON'S LIE: Jefferson increased the number of professorships of divinity at the University of Virginia by inviting the various religious sects to establish their own theological schools at the university. Jefferson was implementing a plan proposed by Rev. Samuel Knox. University students were expected to attend the theological school of their sect.

THE TRUTH: There were no professorships of divinity or theological schools whatsoever at the University of Virginia. Jefferson's invitation to the various sects was simply a plan to stop the attacks by the clergy on the university. None of the sects accepted this invitation. Samuel Knox had absolutely nothing to do with Jefferson's plan. University students could not have been expected to attend the theological school of their sect because these schools did not exist.

Immediately following his lies about Jefferson's *nonpreferentially* promoting Christianity at William and Mary, Barton continues with this:

> **In the same manner Jefferson sought to ensure that the University of Virginia would also reflect denominational nonpreferentialism. He therefore invited the seminaries**

of many denominations to establish themselves on the campus, explaining:

> We suggest the expediency of encouraging the different religious sects [denominations] to establish, each for itself, a professorship of their own tenets, on the confines of the university so near as that their students may attend the lectures there, and have the free use of our library, and every other accommodation we can give them.... [B]y bringing the sects together, and mixing them with the mass of other students, we shall soften their asperities [harshness], liberalize and neutralize their prejudices [prejudgment without an examination of the facts], and make the general religion a religion of peace, reason, and morality.

What Barton is quoting (and heavily editing) here is a letter that Jefferson wrote to Dr. Thomas Cooper in 1822. What Jefferson was writing about in this letter was the end of a story that began two years earlier, so rather than trying to explain what this letter was about here, I'm going to start at the beginning of the story.

Most of the lies about religion at the University of Virginia are created by using one of two documents – the 1818 *Report of the Commissioners appointed to fix the site of the University of Virginia* (often referred to as the Rockfish Report, as it will be here) and the October 1822 report of the university's Board of Visitors to the legislature. The lies are created by quoting things that Jefferson put into these two reports that he never really had any intention of doing once the university opened, and then pretending that he actually did do them once the university opened. The most popular of these lies is that Jefferson established theological schools at the university. He didn't. This is not open to interpretation. These schools simply did not exist. The second most popular of these lies is that there was religious instruction at the university. There wasn't, at least not until decades after Jefferson's death, so Jefferson obviously had nothing to do with it.

In 1818, five years before the university opened, Jefferson had to get the legislature to approve a university that would have no professor of divinity or religious instruction, and in 1822, three years before it opened, he had to stop the attacks that the clergy were waging on the university because the clergy's attacks were being used by his enemies in the legislature to hold up the funding to complete the university's buildings. In both cases, Jefferson had to make it sound like there would be some religion at the university, even though there really wasn't going to be. The records of the university, Jefferson's own correspondence, and articles written at both the time of the university's founding and in the couple of decades that followed all confirm this.

The letter from Jefferson to Thomas Cooper that Barton quotes was about a plan that Jefferson proposed in the 1822 report of the university's Board of Visitors that was designed to stop the attacks by the clergy. The plan was to invite all of the different religious sects to open their own theological schools near the university. This invitation would make it impossible for the clergy to continue claiming that Jefferson's university was going to be a bastion of deism and Unitarianism.

This invitation to the religious sects is the source of a number of variations of the same lie, all of which contain some combination of the following three claims: that the invitation was extended by Jefferson to promote religious instruction at the university; that religious schools were invited by Jefferson to build on government property; and, that these schools were *actually built* and attended by university students, as Barton claims in *The Jefferson Lies*. This invitation to the religious sects is also the plan that Barton claims Jefferson got from Rev. Samuel Knox.

The real story behind the University of Virginia's October 1822 invitation to the religious sects begins over two years earlier. It all started in January 1820, when John Holt Rice, a Presbyterian minister and editor of the *Virginia Literary and Evangelical Magazine,* published an article that, among other things, accused the university of promoting Unitarianism and excluding trinitarian Christianity.

Rice's accusation was based on the appointment of Thomas Cooper as the university's first professor. Dr. Cooper was a Unitarian, and had a reputation for being outspoken about his religious opinions. Rice, assuming that Jefferson would be excluding clergymen from the professorships at the university, claimed that the appointment of Dr. Cooper, although he wasn't a clergyman, was a promotion of Unitarianism. In his preface to an 1806 edition of *The Memoirs of Dr. Joseph Priestley,* Cooper had made some unfavorable statements about trinitarian Christianity. Rice included these shocking statements in his article as proof of Cooper's animosity towards all trinitarian sects. Rice's article was very effective, uniting Virginia's rival Christian sects in a common cause – opposing the appointment of Thomas Cooper as a professor at the university.

Cooper, who was not only an eminent scientist but also a lawyer and former judge, had already accepted the professorship of law and chemistry when the university was still known as Central College, but while waiting for the university to open, had taken a temporary position teaching chemistry at South Carolina College. This is where he was when he first heard about John Holt Rice's article, receiving an extract from it from a friend in Richmond. Cooper had already been the subject of an attack by the clergy in Pennsylvania and knew from experience how ugly this new attack in Virginia was likely to get. So, he wrote to Jefferson in March 1820 and offered to resign from the university if Jefferson thought he should. But Jefferson, who had only heard about Rice's article a few days before receiving Cooper's resignation offer, greatly underestimated the damage it was going to do, and replied to Cooper that the article, in what he considered an obscure periodical, would soon be forgotten. The following, from his reply to Cooper's resignation offer, was Jefferson's initial assessment of the Rice situation.

> The Baptists are sound republicans and zealous supporters of their government. The Methodists are republican mostly, satisfied with their government meddling with nothing but the concerns of their own calling and opposing nothing. These two sects are entirely friendly to our university. The anglicans are the same. The

Presbyterian clergy alone (not their followers) remain bitterly federal and malcontent with their government. They are violent, ambitious of power, and intolerant in politics as in religion and want nothing but license from the laws to kindle again the fires of their leader John Knox, and to give us a 2d blast from his trumpet. Having a little more monkish learning than the clergy of the other sects, they are jealous of the general diffusion of science, and therefore hostile to our Seminary lest it should qualify their antagonists of the other sects to meet them in equal combat. Not daring to attack the institution with the avowal of their real motives, they Peck at you, at me, and every feather they can spy oul. But in this they have no weight, even with their own followers, excepting a few old men among them who may still be federal & Anglomen, their main body are good citizens, friends to their government, anxious for reputation, and therefore friendly to the University.[44]

Jefferson also assumed, based on previous experience, that the other sects would band together against the Presbyterians, regardless of the issue, if it appeared that the Presbyterians were in any way trying to get control of the university. But he soon realized he was wrong about this, writing the following to William Short only a month after his letter to Cooper.

The serious enemies are the priests of the different religious sects, to whose spells on the human mind its improvement is ominous. Their pulpits are now resounding with denunciations against the appointment of Dr. Cooper, whom they charge as a monotheist in opposition to their tritheism. Hostile as these sects are in every other point, to one another, they unite in maintaining their mystical theogony against those who believe there is one God only.[45]

44. Jefferson to Thomas Cooper, March 13, 1820. Adrienne Koch and William Peden, eds., *The Life and Selected Writings of Thomas Jefferson,* (New York: Random House, 1944), 697.

45. Jefferson to William Short, April 13, 1820. Albert Ellery Bergh, ed., *The Writings of Thomas Jefferson,* vol. 15, (Washington D.C.: Thomas Jefferson Memorial Association, 1907), 246.

At the April 1820 meeting of the university's Board of Visitors, a decision was made to renegotiate Cooper's contract, but this was due to the delay in the opening the university, not Dr. Rice's article. At this time, Jefferson worked out a deal with Cooper and still fully intended for him to come to the university as soon as it opened. A year later, however, Cooper was offered the presidency of South Carolina College and decided to accept it. Again, this had nothing to do with the attack started by Rice. It was entirely because of the uncertainty over when the University of Virginia would actually be ready to open. Cooper, whose family was waiting in Pennsylvania because he was unsure about whether to move them to South Carolina or Virginia, needed to make a decision, and the decision he made was to accept the presidency of South Carolina College.

But the attacks begun by John Holt Rice did not end when Cooper decided in 1821 to stay in South Carolina. The rumor that the university was an enemy to all trinitarian sects was just too useful to those who opposed the university for other reasons, particularly those who opposed it out of loyalty to the state's other colleges.

The real issue driving the friends of these other colleges was the amount of money that Jefferson was asking the legislature for. They thought that some of the money from the state's "Literary Fund" should go to the state's other colleges. This led to a second rumor – that Jefferson was being extravagant and wasting public money. This rumor about Jefferson's wasting public money, however, would never have caught on with the public if it hadn't been for the damage already done to the university's reputation by Dr. Rice's attack on Dr. Cooper. So, Jefferson's enemies in the legislature wanted to keep the clergy's attacks on the university going for as long as possible.

The idea of dividing the money in the Literary Fund among all of the state's colleges rather than giving it all to the university was supported mainly by the representatives in the legislature from the areas where these other colleges were located, but it was also supported by some of Jefferson's political enemies, mainly because one of these other schools, Washington College, had strong ties to what remained of Virginia's Federalist party.

Splitting the money in the Literary Fund among all of the state's colleges was also supported by the clergy. The Presbyterians were firmly in control of Hampden-Sidney College, and had plans to establish a theological seminary there. At the same time, the Episcopalians were attempting to reestablish the divinity school at William and Mary that Jefferson had abolished four decades earlier in 1779. Jefferson wasn't overly concerned about the William and Mary supporters in the legislature. It was the supporters of the other colleges, particularly Hampden-Sidney, who were gaining ground, in large part by keeping Dr. Rice's religious attacks on the university alive.

On August 5, 1821, Joseph Cabell, a member of the university's Board of Visitors and also a member of the state legislature, wrote to Jefferson to update him on the situation.

> You, doubtless, observe the movements of the Presbyterians at Hampden Sidney, and the Episcopalians at William & Mary. I learn that the former sect, or rather the clergy of that sect, in their synods and presbyteries, talk much of the University. They believe, as I am informed, that the Socinians are to be installed at the University for the purpose of overthrowing the prevailing religious opinions of the country. They are therefore drawing off, and endeavoring to set up establishments of their own, subject to their own control. Hence the great efforts now making at Hampden Sidney, and the call on all the counties on the south side of James River to unite in support of that college.[46]

In January 1822, Cabell, after consulting with another university board member, Chapman Johnson, decided to try to smooth things over with the clergy. Cabell wrote to Jefferson on January 7 that he intended to talk to Dr. Rice, and also to Bishop Moore, the Episcopalian Bishop who was trying to reestablish the divinity school at William and Mary.

---

46. Joseph C. Cabell to Thomas Jefferson, August 5, 1821. *Early History of the University of Virginia, as Contained in the Letters of Thomas Jefferson and Joseph C. Cabell*, (Richmond, VA: J.W. Randolph, 1856), 215-216.

In reflecting on the causes of the opposition to the University, I cannot but ascribe a great deal of it to the clergy. William & Mary has conciliated them. It is represented that they are to be excluded from the University. There has been no decision to this effect; and, on full reflection, I should suppose that religious opinions should form no test whatever. I should think it improper to exclude religious men, and open the door to such as Doctor Cooper. Mr. Johnson concurs with me in this view. And I have publicly expressed the opinion. The clergy have succeeded in spreading the belief of their intended exclusion, and, in my opinion, it is the source of much of our trouble. I am cautious not to commit yourself, or Mr. Madison, or the board. I have also made overtures of free communication with Mr. Rice, and shall take occasion to call on Bishop Moore. I do not know that I shall touch on this delicate point with either of them. But I wish to consult these heads of the church, and ask their opinions. [47]

It doesn't appear that Joseph Cabell ever met with Bishop Moore, but he did meet with Dr. Rice. Cabell wrote to Jefferson on January 14, 1822 that he thought he had made progress with Rice, but that Rice still wanted a clergyman (even if it was one from another denomination) to be appointed at the university.

I have had a very long interview with Mr. Rice. He and myself differed on some points; but agreed in the propriety of a firm union between the friends of the University and the Colleges, as to measures of common interest, and of postponing for future discussion and settlement points on which we differ. I think this safe ground. We shall be first endowed; and have the vantage ground in this respect....

...They have heard that you have said they may well be afraid of the progress of the Unitarians to the South. This remark was carried

47. Joseph C. Cabell to Thomas Jefferson, January 7, 1822. *Early History of the University of Virginia, as Contained in the Letters of Thomas Jefferson and Joseph C. Cabell,* (Richmond, VA: J.W. Randolph, 1856), 230.

from Bedford to the Synod, beyond the Ridge, last fall. The Bible Societies are in constant correspondence all over the continent, and a fact is wafted across it in a few weeks. Through these societies the discovery of the religious opinions of Ticknor and Bowditch was made. Mr. Rice assured me that he was a warm friend of the University; and that, as a matter of policy, he hoped the Visitors would, in the early stages of its existence, remove the fears of the religious orders. He avowed that the Presbyterians sought no peculiar advantage, and that they and the other sects would be well satisfied by the appointment of an Episcopalian. I stated to him that I knew not what would be the determination of the board; but I was sure no desire existed any where to give any preference to the Unitarians; and, for my own part, I should not vote against any one on account of his being a professor of religion or free-thinker.[48]

The information that Joseph Cabell obtained in his January 1822 meeting with Dr. Rice was probably a bit alarming to Jefferson, particularly that the Presbyterian clergy had heard of his comment about Unitarians from someone in Bedford in the fall. Bedford was the location of Jefferson's second home, Poplar Forest, where he spent time each fall. Jefferson had been writing in letters around this time that Unitarianism was spreading to the south and, in his opinion, would soon be the predominant religion of the country, so it is quite probable that he had also said things to this effect in conversation while in Bedford. The fact that Dr. Rice knew about anything Jefferson had said in Bedford would mean that the clergy had people there reporting what Jefferson was saying, most likely through the network of Bible societies that were known to be used to relay information.

Cabell's other disturbing piece of information from his meeting with Dr. Rice was that the religious opinions of George Ticknor and Nathaniel Bowditch had been investigated. At their October 1820

48. Joseph C. Cabell to Jefferson, January 14, 1822. *Early History of the University of Virginia, as Contained in the Letters of Thomas Jefferson and Joseph C. Cabell*, (Richmond, VA: J.W. Randolph, 1856), 233-237.

meeting, the university's Board of Visitors had passed a resolution to begin negotiations with Ticknor, who was then a professor at Harvard, a school that had been under Unitarian control since 1805, and Bowditch, who was a member of a Unitarian church in Massachusetts. Finding out from Rice that these two candidates for professorships had been investigated by the clergy was a pretty clear sign that every candidate the university was even considering was going to be subjected to a religious test by the Presbyterians. Clearly, hiring *any* Unitarian in the wake of the Thomas Cooper controversy was going to be used by the clergy as proof that Rice's accusation that the university was showing a preference for Unitarians was true.

It was at this point that Jefferson must have realized that Dr. Cooper's decision to stay at South Carolina College was not going to be enough to make the clergy back off and that he was going to have to do something more. The something more that Jefferson came up with was the idea of inviting the various religious sects to open their own theological schools near the university.

Before getting into the details of Jefferson's invitation to the religious sects, we need to stop for one of the biggest whoppers in Barton's chapter.

Having just read what John Holt Rice *really* did, and knowing that Rice not only took part in the attacks on the university but was actually the person who *instigated* the attacks, take a look at what Barton has to say about him:

> **[Jefferson's] nondenominational approach caused Presbyterians, Baptists, Methodists, and others to give the university the friendship and cooperative support necessary to make it a success. Consider Presbyterian minister John Holt Rice as an example.**
>
> **Holt (*sic*) was a nationally known evangelical leader with extensive credentials. He founded the Virginia Bible Society, started the *Virginia Evangelical and Literary Magazine* to report on revivals across the country, was elected national**

leader of the Presbyterian Church, and offered the presidency of Princeton (but instead accepted the chair of theology at Hampton-Sydney College). Rice fully supported and promoted the University of Virginia, but this would not have been the case had the university been perceived to have been affiliated with just one denomination. As Rice explained:

> The plan humbly suggested is to allow Jews, Catholics, Protestants, Episcopalians, Methodists, Baptists, any and all sects, if they shall choose to exercise the privilege, to endow Professorships, and nominate their respective professors. ... [T]he students shall regularly attend Divine worship, but in what form should be left to the direction of parents; or in failure of this, to the choice of the students. In addition to this, the professors in every case must be men of the utmost purity of moral principle and strictness of moral conduct.

Now, besides Barton's completely untrue statement that "Rice fully supported and promoted the University of Virginia," look at the way he presents what he quotes from Rice – saying "As Rice explained," rather than as Rice *proposed.* Barton puts this quote from Rice right after his quote from the university's 1822 report inviting the religious sects to open their own theological schools, making it appear that what Rice was writing about was the 1822 "plan humbly suggested" by Jefferson. But what Barton is actually quoting here was the "plan humbly suggested" by Rice himself – in 1818, four years *before* Jefferson's invitation to the religious sects. What Jefferson did in 1822 was to throw Rice's own proposal from his 1818 article back in his face.

In this article, Rice was writing about his travels through Virginia in October of 1818. This was two months after the meeting of the commissioners who wrote the *Rockfish Report.* That report, which we'll get into a bit later, was the report in which Jefferson first said that the university would have no professor of divinity. At the time that Rice wrote his article, it was already assumed that Jefferson's Central College was going to be selected by the legislature to be the University of Virginia, even though this hadn't been made official yet.

Jefferson's 1822 invitation to the religious sects was essentially what John Holt Rice – the man who started the attacks on the university in 1820 – had proposed in his own article four years earlier. Jefferson was clearly the member of the university's Board of Visitors whose idea it was to invite the religious sects to open their own theological schools, but in the report to the legislature he said it was "suggested by some pious individuals." He might as well have said it was the proposal suggested in the 1818 article by the *pious individual* named John Holt Rice. What better way to stop the attacks of John Holt Rice than to propose the very same plan that Rice himself had proposed in 1818? How could Rice possibly continue to keep up his attacks when Jefferson had just offered him what he had claimed he wanted?

If you read a bit more of Rice's 1818 article, you'll see that as early as October 1818 – well over a year before the January 1820 launch of his attack on Thomas Cooper – Rice was already beginning to raise concerns among the readers of his magazine that Jefferson's university might "exclude Christianity" and be a "Deistical, or Atheistical University."

Stop and think about this for a minute. The whole premise of Barton's *The Jefferson Lies* is that it's only modern academics and secularists who claim that Jefferson was a deist who excluded religion from public institutions. But here we have John Holt Rice, a prominent Presbyterian minister in Virginia at the time that Jefferson was founding the University of Virginia, saying that Jefferson was going to exclude Christianity from the university, exclude clergymen as professors, and that the university was going to be deistical or atheistical. Obviously, John Holt Rice didn't get these ideas about Jefferson from the modern academics who Barton claims are just making all this up. This was the general opinion about Jefferson in his own day!

Take a look at these other quotes from Rice's 1818 article, starting where he begins the part about religion at the university:

> But what will they do in relation to the delicate and important subject of religion? Will an attempt be made to exclude its influences? This is impossible. Man can as soon pull the moon from its orbit, as alter the fundamental and original principles of his nature, so as to free himself from the influences of religion in some form or other. And as surely as the University of Virginia shall be established, it will, in a short time, assume a decided character in this respect – it will be either *Deistical,* or *Socinian,* or *Christian.* ...

> ... Should it finally be decided to exclude Christianity, the opinion will at once be fixed that the institution is infidel – Men according to their prejudices will affix to it different epithets – Some will call it the Socinian; others, the Deistical, or Atheistical University.[49]

After sounding the alarm bells that a university run by Jefferson might being deistical or atheistical, Rice proposed *his* solution, which is what Barton was quoting. But Barton omitted a few words from this quote (which are bolded here) because these words make it obvious that Rice wasn't writing about Jefferson's 1822 invitation to the religious sects, but was proposing his incredibly similar idea at some point before Jefferson extended his invitation.

> The plan humbly suggested is to allow Jews, Catholics, Protestants, Episcopalians, Methodists, Baptists, any and all sects, if they shall choose to exercise the privilege, to endow Professorships, and nominate their respective professors. **Let it also be a statute of the University, that** the students shall regularly attend divine worship; but in what form should be left to the direction of parents; or in failure of this, to the choice of the students.[50]

49. John Holt Rice, "An Excursion Into the Country," *The Virginia Evangelical and Literary Magazine,* vol 1, (Richmond, VA: William W. Gray, 1818), 547.
50. Ibid., 548.

When Jefferson decided to extend this invitation to the religious sects, it was possible, although not likely, that they would actually accept it. The Presbyterians were already establishing their seminary at Hampton-Sydney, the Episcopalians were busy trying to reestablish the divinity school at William and Mary that Jefferson himself had abolished over four decades earlier. The other two big denominations in Virginia, the Baptists and the Methodists, just hadn't shown any interest in opening schools before, so there was no reason to think they would suddenly want to open schools just because of the university's invitation. But even though it wasn't likely, it was always possible that one or more of the sects might actually decide to take the university up on its offer. In his letters to Thomas Cooper (who he continued to write to about the university even though Cooper had decided to stay at South Carolina College), Jefferson explained why he extended the invitation, what he thought the likelihood of any of the sects accepting it was, and how effective the invitation was at stopping the clergy's attacks on the university.

Jefferson's letters to Cooper might seem to contradict each other – at one point saying it was possible that all the sects might accept the invitation, at another point saying that there was only one sect that might accept it, and at another saying that none of them would accept it – but what seem like contradictions were really just Jefferson trying to predict what would happen based on the best information he had about what the Presbyterians and the Episcopalians were up to at the time he wrote each letter.

What needs to be understood is that the sect that Jefferson was really worried about was the Presbyterians, who had a long track record of taking over colleges and turning them into Presbyterian institutions. Jefferson knew that if the Presbyterians did decide to open a school near the university, then the other sects might also want to open schools for no other reason than to prevent a possible Presbyterian takeover of their state university.

By April 1823, six months after extending the invitation, Jefferson was pretty sure that none of the sects was going to accept it, although, as he wrote to Thomas Cooper, there was still a possibility that the Episcopalians might. By this time, Jefferson was no longer worried about the Presbyterians. This meant that the Baptists and the Methodists were also out of the picture, since the only reason they might want to open schools would be if the Presbyterians did. But the reason he didn't completely rule out the Episcopalians at this time was that he knew that their attempt to reestablish the divinity school at William and Mary had been deemed a failure at the end of 1822, having attracted only one student in two years. As of April 1823, they were looking for another location to try again. Although they eventually selected Alexandria as the location for their second attempt, this was still up in the air when Jefferson wrote his letter to Cooper, so it was still possible at that point that they might decide to relocate near the university.

In the end, Jefferson's plan did work. Joseph Cabell, with a reference to Benjamin Franklin's invention of the lightning rod, called the invitation to the religious sects "the Franklin that has drawn the lightning from the cloud of opposition." To battle the other problematic rumor – that Jefferson was wasting public money – Cabell suggested that the board have a set of books prepared for the legislature, accounting for every penny that had been spent.

In February 1823, when it looked certain that an important bill was going to be passed by the legislature and funding for the university would no longer be held up, Cabell wrote to Jefferson:

> I was, from the first, confident that no weapon could be wielded by us with more efficacy than this annual rendition of accounts which seemed to be a rod in pickle for us. I think also that your suggestion respecting the religious sects has had great influence. It is the Franklin that has drawn the lightning from the cloud of opposition. I write you, dear sir, with a heart springing up with joy, and a cheek bedewed with tears of delight. Accept, I beseech you, my cordial congratulations at this evidence of the returning good sense of the country, and of its just appreciation of your labors. [51]

51. Joseph C. Cabell to Thomas Jefferson, February 3, 1823. *Early History of the University of Virginia, as Contained in the Letters of Thomas Jefferson and Joseph C. Cabell*, (Richmond, VA: J.W. Randolph, 1856), 273.

So, having now read a little more about Jefferson's invitation to the religious sects, and what led up to his extending this invitation, take another look at what Barton wrote at the beginning of this section:

In the same manner Jefferson sought to ensure that the University of Virginia would also reflect denominational nonpreferentialism. He therefore invited the seminaries of many denominations to establish themselves on the campus, explaining:

> **We suggest the expediency of encouraging the different religious sects [denominations] to establish, each for itself, a professorship of their own tenets, on the confines of the university so near as that their students may attend the lectures there, and have the free use of our library, and every other accommodation we can give them.... [B]y bringing the sects together, and mixing them with the mass of other students, we shall soften their asperities [harshness], liberalize and neutralize their prejudices [prejudgment without an examination of the facts], and make the general religion a religion of peace, reason, and morality.**

What Barton is quoting from here is Jefferson's November 1822 letter to Thomas Cooper.

Here's a bit more of that letter – a letter that includes what Jefferson really thought about the Presbyterians, and his famous (but wrong) prediction that Unitarianism would become the majority religion of the country. The section quoted by Barton is, of course, unedited here. The part removed by Barton is in bold.

Their [the Presbyterians] ambition and tyranny would tolerate no rival if they had power. Systematical in grasping at an ascendency over all other sects, they aim, like the Jesuits, at engrossing the education of the country, are hostile to every institution which they do not direct, and jealous at seeing others begin to attend at all to that object. The diffusion of instruction, to which there is now so growing an attention, will be the remote remedy to this fever of fanaticism; while the more proximate one will be the progress of Unitarianism. That this will, ere long, be the religion of the majority from North to South, I have no doubt.

In our university you know there is no Professorship of Divinity. A handle has been made of this, to disseminate an idea that this is an institution, not merely of no religion, but against all religion. Occasion was taken at the last meeting of the Visitors, to bring forward an idea that might silence this calumny, which weighed on the minds of some honest friends to the institution. In our annual report to the legislature, after stating the constitutional reasons against a public establishment of any religious instruction, we suggest the expediency of encouraging the different religious sects to establish, each for itself, a professorship of their own tenets, on the confines of the university, so near as that their students may attend the lectures there, and have the free use of our library, and every other accommodation we can give them; **preserving, however, their independence of us and of each other. This fills the chasm objected to ours, as a defect in an institution professing to give instruction in *all* useful sciences. I think the invitation will be accepted, by some sects from candid intentions, and by others from jealousy and rivalship. And** by bringing the sects together, and mixing them with the mass of other students, we shall soften their asperities, liberalize and neutralize their prejudices, and make the general religion a religion of peace, reason, and morality.[52]

And this is from Jefferson's April 1823 letter to Cooper, written shortly after Jefferson learned from Joseph Cabell that the invita-

---

52. Jefferson to Thomas Cooper, November 2, 1822. Albert Ellery Bergh, ed., *The Writings of Thomas Jefferson,* vol. 15, (Washington D.C.: Thomas Jefferson Memorial Association, 1907), 404-406.

tion had, in fact, been effective in stopping the use of the clergy's rumors by the university's enemies in the legislature.

> ... their effort has been to represent ours as an anti-religious insti-
> tution. we disarmed them of this calumny however in our last
> report by inviting the different sects to establish their respective
> divinity schools on the margin of the grounds of the University, so
> that their students might attend its schools & have the benefit of
> its library, to be entirely independent of it at the same time, and no
> ways incorporated with it. one sect [the Episcopalians], I think,
> may do it, but another [the Presbyterians], disdaining equality,
> ambitioning nothing less than a soaring ascendancy, will despise
> our invitation. they are hostile to all educ^n of which they have not
> the direction, and foresee that this inst^n, by enlightening the minds
> of the people and encouraging them to appeal to their own common
> sense is to dispel the fanaticism on which their power is built.[53]

As you can see, Barton just completely ignores everything in Jefferson's letters where he made it perfectly clear that the reason for his invitation to the religious sects was to stop the clergy's attacks on the university. Obviously, these letters would really screw up Barton's story about all that "friendship and cooperative support" the university got from the clergy. And, of course, the fact that the reason for the attacks was that the clergy of Jefferson's own time thought that he was founding a "deistical" or "atheistical" university pretty much blows the whole claim that Jefferson didn't found a secular university out of the water – unless Barton is going to say that the clergy of nineteenth century Virginia were lying.

Now, there's one more thing that we need to jump back to from the beginning of this section. Remember how Barton claimed at the beginning that Jefferson got his idea for the university's invitation to the religious sects from Rev. Samuel Knox? To refresh your mem-

---

53. Jefferson to Thomas Cooper, April 12, 1823. *The Thomas Jefferson Papers, Series 1, General Correspondence, 1651-1827*, Library of Congress Manuscript Division.

ory, here's what Barton wrote again:

In 1799 the Rev. Knox penned a policy paper proposing the formation of a state university that would invite many denominations to establish multiple theological schools rather than just one, so they would work together in mutual Christian cooperation rather than competition. Jefferson agreed with Knox's philosophy, and it was this model that he employed at his University of Virginia.

Knowing now that Jefferson's idea to extend the invitation to the religious sects was actually Jefferson proposing the same plan that John Holt Rice had proposed in his 1818 article, it's pretty obvious that the 1799 paper written by Rev. Samuel Knox had nothing to do with Jefferson's idea. And, besides that, Knox's plan really had nothing in common with Jefferson's 1822 invitation.

Knox did not propose "the formation of a state university that would invite many denominations to establish multiple theological schools," as Barton claims. Barton is just changing Knox's plan to make it sound like Jefferson's invitation.

What Knox proposed, as part of a national education plan, was that each denomination have one seminary somewhere in each state, not that the religious schools of the different denominations would all be near their state university. In Knox's plan, students who intended to study for the ministry would go on to these seminaries to study theology *after* getting their general, non-religious education at the public university of their state.[54] This was nothing at all like the invitation extended by Jefferson, which was for the various denominations to all establish their seminaries near the university so that ministry students could attend their theological seminary and the university at the same time.

Since Barton is claiming that the invitation to the religious sects was something that Jefferson genuinely wanted to do, rather

---

54. Samuel Knox, *An Essay on the Best System of Liberal Education, Adapted to the Genius of the Government of the United States,* (Baltimore: Warner & Hanna, 1799), 78.

than something he had to do to put a stop to the clergy's attacks, he goes on to list all the benefits that Jefferson thought would come of this great idea.

> **Jefferson observed that a positive benefit of this approach was that it would "give the sectarians schools of divinity the full benefit of the public [university] provisions made for instruction" and "leave every sect to provide as they think fittest the means of further instruction in their own peculiar tenets." Jefferson pointed out that another benefit of this arrangement was that students could "attend religious exercises with the professor of their particular sect," and he made clear that students would be fully *expected* to actively participate in some denominational school.**

Wow! From all of that – especially the thing about students at the university being "expected" to participate in one of these theological schools – you might think that these schools actually existed. Barton just never gets around to letting his readers know that none of the religious sects ever took the university up on its invitation. There were no theological schools!

Barton gets this thing about students being "fully expected" to attend these nonexistent theological schools from the university's rules, written in 1824. Even though it was clear by the time these rules were written that there weren't actually going to be any theological schools, the rules said that if any of the religious sects did decide to establish a school, the students would be "expected to attend religious worship at the establishment of their respective sects, in the morning, and in time to meet their school in the University at its stated hour." [55] Unless Jefferson was expecting students to "actively participate" in schools that didn't actually exist, this seems to be a rule saying what time of day the students would be allowed to attend religious worship if there ever were such schools

---

55. Albert Ellery Bergh, ed., *The Writings of Thomas Jefferson*, vol. 19, (Washington D.C.: Thomas Jefferson Memorial Association, 1907), 449.

in the future, and that attending religious worship would not be an excuse to be late for classes.

Barton next goes on to claim that Jefferson increased the number of professors of divinity at the university.

Jefferson and the Visitors (regents) also decided that there should be no clergyman as president and no Professor of Divinity because it might give the impression that the university favored the denomination with which the university president or professor of divinity was affiliated. But the fact that the school did not have a specific professor of divinity did not mean that it was secular.

In fact, Jefferson actually increased the number of Professorships of Divinity by encouraging each denomination to have "a professorship of their own tenets" at the school.

Again, there were *no* professors of divinity at the university because there were *no* theological schools. You can't increase something that there are none of to begin with! What Barton is doing here is quoting that same letter Jefferson wrote to Thomas Cooper in November 1822 in which Jefferson was talking about the invitation to the religious sects. In that letter, Jefferson referred to the hypothetical professors of each of the nonexistent theological seminaries as "a professorship of their own tenets." Barton just reuses that same letter, this time plucking a different snippet from it, and makes it sound as if this were some separate thing that Jefferson did that "increased the number of Professorships of Divinity."

While Barton's chapter has a whole separate section about all the alleged religious instruction that took place at the university, he throws the following claim about the university's professor of ethics into this section, so we'll knock this one off here.

And the decision not to have just one exclusive professor of divinity also did not mean that the university would have no religious instruction. To the contrary, Jefferson

personally directed that the teaching of "the proofs of the being of a God, the Creator, Preserver, and Supreme Ruler of the Universe, the Author of all the relations of morality and of the laws and obligations these infer, will be within the province of the Professor of Ethics."

What Barton is quoting here is the *Rockfish Report*. As explained earlier, this was the 1818 report where Jefferson, who was trying to get Central College approved as the state university, had to get the legislature to approve a university that would have no professor of divinity – and he needed to do it without its sounding like there wouldn't be any religious instruction at all. One of the things he threw in to accomplish this was making it sound like the ethics professor was going to be teaching some religion.

But Jefferson never really intended to have the ethics professor teaching religion. This is absolutely clear from the correspondence between Jefferson and Board of Visitors member James Madison when they were actually looking for an ethics professor in 1824. Nowhere in any of Jefferson's or Madison's letters is a knowledge of religion, or even having a religion, ever considered as a qualification for the ethics professorship. In fact, they didn't even care if the ethics professor had any qualifications to teach ethics. That's because they really weren't looking for an ethics professor.

Because the university's charter limited them to ten professors, and finances to even fewer than that, what Jefferson and Madison were really looking for was a professor who could teach some other subject or subjects. This professor would have to teach a bit of ethics, since the *Rockfish Report* said they were going to have an ethics professor, but this would be secondary to whatever other subject or subjects he taught.

This is from Jefferson's first letter to Madison on the subject:

I am quite at a loss for a Professor of Ethics. This subject has been so exclusively confined to the clergy, that when forced to seek one, not of that body, it becomes difficult. But it is a branch of science of little difficulty to any ingenious man. Locke, Stewart,

Brown, Tracy for the general science of the mind furnish material abundant, and that of Ethics is still more trite. I should think that any person, with a general education rendering them otherwise worthy of a place among his scientific brethren might soon qualify himself.[56]

Madison replied by suggesting George Tucker, a lawyer, political economist, and member of Congress.

What are the collateral aptitudes of George Tucker the member of Congress. I have never seen him, and can only judge him by a volume of miscellaneous Essays published not very long ago. They are written with acuteness and elegance; and indicate a capacity and taste for Philosophical literature.[57]

The two possibilities that Jefferson was thinking about before Madison suggested George Tucker were also lawyers.

It's quite apparent from their letters that neither Jefferson nor Madison knew enough about George Tucker to have any idea whether he was religious or not, let alone qualified to teach about religion. Their opinion that he was qualified for this professorship was based solely on a collection of fifteen essays, none of which had anything to do with religion. The wide variety of topics covered in Tucker's essay collection included the evolution of language, why Americans were not advancing in literature as quickly as they were advancing in science, why Greek architecture had remained so popular through the centuries, whether or not poetry should rhyme, the pros and cons of an increase in population, and a justification of the practice of dueling.

Among Tucker's scientific interests was mental philosophy, the forerunner to psychology. Tucker's particular areas of research in this field while a professor at the University of Virginia included memory,

---

56. Jefferson to James Madison, November 30, 1824. James Morton Smith, ed., *The Republic of Letters: The Correspondence Between Thomas Jefferson and James Madison 1776-1826,* vol. 3, (New York and London: W.W. Norton & Company, 1995), 1909.

57. James Madison to Jefferson, December 3, 1824. Ibid., 1910.

the association of ideas, and the similarities and differences between waking thought and dreams. He also conducted a nature vs. nurture study using the famous Siamese twins, Chang and Eng, as subjects.

But what probably made Tucker most appealing to Jefferson and Madison was that he was an expert in the field of economics, which back then was called *political economy*.

When Tucker was offered the professorship in January 1825, he didn't immediately accept it. The previous summer he had written *Valley of the Shenandoah*, a tragic novel about a southern plantation family. Tucker had hoped to begin a career as a full-time novelist when his term in Congress was over, but this plan wasn't going very well. Although his novel was later reprinted in England and translated into German, only a hundred copies were printed in America, and Tucker himself had to put up half the money for the printing. So, when his term in Congress ended in March 1825, Tucker decided to accept the professorship, which would give him a house and a salary, while leaving him enough time to pursue his career as a novelist. Two years later, under the pseudonym Joseph Atterley, Tucker published his second novel, *A Voyage to the Moon with Some Account of the Manners and Customs, Science and Philosophy, of the People of Morosofia, and Other Lunarians,* a satirical science fiction novel about a trip to the moon in a spaceship coated with an anti-gravity metal, in which Tucker "aimed to notice the errors of the day in science and philosophy."

Because of the limited number of professors they could hire, the Board of Visitors assigned several subjects to each professor, but allowed for the subjects to be rearranged in the future based on the particular qualifications of each professor. As of 1824, the ethics professor, who was by then being called the Professor of Moral Philosophy, was to teach "mental science generally, including ideology, general grammar and ethics."[58] Political economy had originally been assigned to the professor of law, but was handed over to Tucker. Tucker also picked up rhetoric and *belles lettres*,

---

58. Albert Ellery Bergh, ed., *The Writings of Thomas Jefferson*, vol. 19, (Washington D.C.: Thomas Jefferson Memorial Association, 1907), 434.

which had previously been assigned to the Professor of Ancient Languages.

Apparently, by the time the university actually opened, Jefferson had forgotten all about that line he had stuck in the *Rockfish Report* six years earlier about the ethics professor teaching "the proofs of the being of a God, the Creator, Preserver, and Supreme Ruler of the Universe, the Author of all the relations of morality and of the laws and obligations these infer."

Nothing whatsoever about George Tucker's position, which ended up being named Professor of Moral Philosophy and Political Economy, was religious. But this doesn't stop Barton from claiming that Jefferson "personally directed" this professor to teach religion.

Okay, we're at the end of another section, so it's recap time again. In this section Barton claimed that:

1. Jefferson promoted Christianity at the College of William and Mary when he was on its Board of Visitors in 1779. Barton's *proof* of this is that the school had a missionary to the Indians.

Reality: Jefferson abolished all religious education at the College of William and Mary, and he transformed the college's pre-existing religious mission to the Indians into an anthropological mission to study the culture and languages of the Indians.

2. Rev. John Holt Rice supported the University of Virginia.

Reality: Rev. John Holt Rice was actually the guy who launched the attacks on the university, which he said was going to be a "deistical" or "atheistical" school.

3. Jefferson established multiple theological schools at the University of Virginia and expected university students to attend these theological schools. Jefferson based these theological schools on a plan proposed by Rev. Samuel Knox in 1799 .

Reality: No theological schools were ever established at the University of Virginia. Students could not have been expected to attend these theological schools because these schools didn't exist. Jefferson's plan for these nonexistent theological schools had nothing to do with Rev. Samuel Knox's plan. He extended an invitation to the religious sects to open their own schools near the university to put a stop to the attacks by the clergy on the university.

4. Jefferson wanted Rev. Samuel Knox to be a professor at the University of Virginia.

Reality: Jefferson did not want any clergymen as professors at the university, and even went as far as lying to Rev. Samuel Knox to keep him from trying to get a professorship at the university.

5. Jefferson increased the number of professors of divinity at the University of Virginia.

Reality: Jefferson couldn't have increased the number of professors of divinity at the University of Virginia because there were *no* professors of divinity at the university. There were no professors of divinity at the university was because there were no theological schools at the university for them to be professors of.

6. Jefferson directed the University of Virginia's professor of ethics to teach religion.

Reality: There was absolutely nothing religious about any of the courses taught by the ethics professor at the University of Virginia. The man chosen for this position was a lawyer, former congressman, and political economist, and had absolutely no qualifications to teach religion.

Barton adds one final piece of *evidence* at the end of this section. He presents what he calls the "university's founding prayer." But if you look up what this prayer was you'll find that it was just the prayer from the freemasons' cornerstone laying ceremony for Central College in 1817, and not any kind of official prayer of the University of Virginia.

But, based on all the claims above that aren't true, here's how Barton concludes this section of his book:

> **Clearly, then, Jefferson's own writings and the records of the University, along with the explanations given by ministers who supported the school, all absolutely refute any notion that the University of Virginia was a secular institution. Instead it was the nation's first prominent transdenominational school.**

Obviously, Barton has proven nothing of the kind in the section of his book from which he draws this conclusion.

What "Jefferson's own writings and the records of the University" show is the exact opposite of what Barton claims they show.

And, if you noticed, ministers became plural in Barton's conclusion, where he says "explanations given by ministers who supported the school." But he only wrote about one minister as a supporter of the school, and that one minister was John Holt Rice, who was anything but a supporter of the school. He then claims that the writings of these now plural ministers "all absolutely refute any notion that the University of Virginia was a secular institution." But it was John Holt Rice, the only one of these plural ministers he actually wrote about, who said that the university was going to be "deistical" or "atheistical." Rice didn't "refute" this *notion;* he promoted it!

Every single one of Barton's claims in this section is a lie. But he's not even close to being done yet. We still have three sections to go.

2. Was Jefferson's Faculty Composed of Unitarians?

Barton's question #2 is nothing but a straw man. Barton managed to find one recent author inaccurately saying that the University of Virginia's faculty were all deists and Unitarians, and presents this one obscure author's erroneous statement as if it were some kind of current widespread belief about Jefferson that he needs to debunk. The claim that Jefferson hired only deists and Unitarians hasn't been a serious question since the time of the university's founding, when people believed the rumors started by John Holt Rice in 1820.

So, who is this modern author who said that Jefferson's faculty were all deists and Unitarians? Must have been some anti-Christian liberal professor, right? Well, no. It was a guy named Daryl Cornett, who used to be an assistant professor of church history at the Mid-America Theological Seminary and is now the senior pastor of a Baptist church. Cornett is one of four professors whom Barton quotes at the beginning of his chapter as examples of the "modern academics" whose claims he's going to debunk. Here's what Barton quotes from Cornett:

Jefferson also founded the first intentionally secularized university in America. His vision for the University of Virginia was for education finally free from traditional Christian dogma. He had a disdain for the influence that institutional Christianity had on education. At the University of

Virginia there was no Christian curriculum and the school had no chaplain. Its faculty were religiously Deists and Unitarians.

– Professor Daryl Cornett,
Mid-America Theological Seminary

No historian who has studied the history of the University of Virginia would ever say that Jefferson only hired deists and Unitarians to teach there – because he didn't. But Cornett is not an historian, unless you count church history. He has a Master of Divinity and a Ph.D. in church history from the Southern Baptist Theological Seminary. And Cornett is certainly not someone who is widely read or considered any kind of authority on Jefferson. In fact, in a decade of studying and writing about the founders and religion, I'd never even heard of Daryl Cornett, let alone read anything written by him.

Oddly, the book that Barton's Daryl Cornett quote comes from is one that Barton himself contributed to. The book, titled *Christian America? Perspectives on Our Religious Heritage,* was published in 2011 by B&H Publishing Group, a division of LifeWay Christian Resources. This is the publishing arm of the Southern Baptist Convention, and "exists to provide intentional, Bible-centered content that positively impacts the hearts and minds of people, inspiring them to build a lifelong relationship with Jesus Christ."

The book consists of essays on the issue of church/state separation by four authors, all of them Christians, with each author expressing a different viewpoint on whether or not America is a Christian nation. Barton's viewpoint is, of course, that America is "distinctly Christian," while Cornett's essay takes the middle ground of America being "partially Christian." The book also includes responses from each of its four authors to the essays of the other three. Only one of the other authors goes far enough for Barton. Even Cornett – a Baptist pastor who taught at a conservative Baptist seminary whose website lists events like trips to the Creation Museum in Kentucky – is too secular for Barton.

As I said, Cornett is wrong about Jefferson's only hiring deists and Unitarians as professors at the University of Virginia (although the rest of what he said is correct). But, as I also said, Cornett is not considered by anybody to be any kind of authority on Jefferson, and his erroneous statement in an obscure book of essays is not going to influence any real historians or lead a whole bunch of other academics to repeat what he said. Barton just uses this quote from an obscure author in an obscure book as an example of what all "modern academics" are saying to erect his straw man.

But, even though Barton is absolutely right about Jefferson's not hiring Unitarians as professors, his section "debunking" this straw man *still* contains a couple of lies. This guy apparently just can't help himself.

The biggest lie in this section is one regarding Dr. Thomas Cooper, the Unitarian targeted by John Holt Rice's attacks on the university. But before getting to that one, let's take a look at the quotes Barton uses to knock down his straw man.

Barton gets these quotes from the two original University of Virginia professors from Henry S. Randall's 1858 Jefferson biography *The Life of Thomas Jefferson,* but the editing of them was done by Barton.

> **Jefferson established ten teaching positions at the university, and *none* of the professors filling them was a Unitarian. In fact, when two of the original professors (George Tucker, professor of moral philosophy, and Robley Dunglison, professor of anatomy and medicine) were later asked whether Jefferson had sought to fill the faculty with Deists or Unitarians, Professor Dunglison succinctly answered:**
>
> > I have not the slightest reason for believing that Mr. Jefferson was, in any respect, guided in his selection of Professors of the University of Virginia by religious considerations. ... In all my conversations with Mr. Jefferson, no reference was made to the subject. I was an Episcopalian so was Mr. Tucker, Mr. Long, Mr. Key, Mr. Bonnycastle, and Dr. Emmet.

117

Dr. Blaetterman, I think, was a Lutheran; but I do not know so much about his religion as I do about that of the rest. There certainly was *not* a Unitarian among us. (emphasis added)

Professor Tucker agreed, declaring:

I believe that all the first Professors belonged to the Episcopal Church, except Dr. Blaetterman, who, I believe, was a German Lutheran. ... I don't remember that I ever heard the religious creeds of either Professors or Visitors [Regents] discussed or inquired into by Mr. Jefferson, or any one else.

What Barton omits from the Robley Dunglison quote is minor. Dunglison said it was actually Francis Gilmer who had picked all the professors who came from Europe, and that it was Gilmer who hadn't asked about their religious beliefs. Jefferson sent Gilmer to Europe in 1824 to hire professors, and the only known instruction he gave him regarding religion was "no clergymen."[59] Jefferson imposed no religious test beyond that, which he himself said would have been unconstitutional. It is odd, however, that Gilmer didn't recruit a single Presbyterian. Apparently, Jefferson forgot to tell Gilmer how much he loved those Presbyterians and their Scottish Common Sense.

The notable thing in the letters Barton quotes is the revelation that only one of the university's original professors appears to have been more than only nominally religious. But, you wouldn't know that from reading Barton's book. That's because Barton removes the part of George Tucker's letter that says it. While Barton's omission in the Robley Dunglison quote is minor, his omission in the George Tucker quote is not. The only explanation for this omission is that Barton is trying to make the university's original professors sound more religious than they actually were.

59. Agenda for the University of Virginia, April 26, 1824. *The Thomas Jefferson Papers, Series 1, General Correspondence, 1651-1827*, Library of Congress Manuscript Division.

Here is the entire excerpt from Tucker's letter as it appears in the source cited by Barton, Randall's biography of Jefferson, with Barton's omission in bold.

> I am not able to give you all the information you require relative to the first Visitors and Professors of the University. The Visitors, I believe were Messrs. Jefferson, Madison, Monroe, Chapman Johnson, Joseph C. Cabell, Gen. John H. Cocke, and George Loyall. But I am not able to say whether they were Unitarians or Trinitarians. I believe that all the first Professors belonged to the Episcopal Church, except Dr. Blaetterman, who, I believe, was a German Lutheran; **but I think there was no one except Mr. Lomax, the Professor of Law, and now a judge, who was a communicant.** I don't remember that I ever heard the religious creeds of either Professors or Visitors discussed or inquired into by Mr. Jefferson, or any one else. [60]

Throughout *The Jefferson Lies* and in his other writings, Barton, who incessantly claims to use only original sources, relies heavily on Randall's 1858 biography of Jefferson. This brings us to a very important thing that needs to be understood about Jefferson biographies, which I might as well explain here since Barton's use of Randall's work is a great example to illustrate the problem.

In looking at different biographies and other writings about Jefferson over the years, what needs to be kept in mind is that the attitude towards Jefferson changed dramatically in the mid-nineteenth century. While Jefferson was alive, and for about two decades after his death, people just accepted that he wasn't a Christian and that his policies in government and education were secular.

Prior to the mid-1800s there were still a lot people around who were alive when Jefferson was alive. These people had read what the newspapers and magazines said about Jefferson during his lifetime. They knew what Jefferson was really like when it came to religion.

---

60. Henry S. Randall, *The Life of Thomas Jefferson,* vol. 3, (New York, Derby & Jackson, 1858), 467.

Jefferson was as familiar to them as our current public figures are to us. We know which ones want to mix religion and government and which ones get bashed by the anti-church/state separation crowd for being secularists, and so did the people of Jefferson's day. They knew Jefferson's reputation as an unreligious secularist and just wouldn't have believed anyone who tried to portray him as some kind of traditional Christian (or even a Christian at all) or said that his views on government and education were anything other than entirely secular. Therefore, people writing about Jefferson didn't even attempt to paint him as more religious or less secular than he really was. Unlike today, those who disagreed with Jefferson's secularism didn't try to revise history. They acknowledged that he *was* a secularist and attacked him for it, saying that he was wrong and that his secular policies should be changed.

For example, in the 1840s, after Jefferson (who died in 1826) and Madison (who died in 1836) were both gone, the people who had disagreed with the secular policies at the University of Virginia didn't deny that Jefferson had founded a secular university. What they did was begin a campaign to remake the university into the religious institution that they thought it should be. We'll get into this more in the next section for a different reason, but for now I just want to use a few quotes from the 1840s to show how Jefferson's policies at the University of Virginia were written about prior to the 1850s.

One of the advocates of the movement that began in the 1840s to religify the University of Virginia was a Presbyterian minister named James W. Alexander. Here is what Alexander wrote to his fellow Presbyterian minister John Hall in 1840, when Jefferson and Madison were gone and it was beginning to look like a religious takeover of the university might be possible:

> The religious prospects of the University of Virginia are really encouraging. It seems as if Providence was throwing contempt on old Jefferson's ashes.[61]

---

61. James W. Alexander to John Hall, June 10, 1840. John Hall, D.D., ed., *Forty Years' Familiar Letters of James W. Alexander, D.D.*, vol. 1, (New York: Charles Scribner, 1860), 305.

An 1842 article about the university in the *Southern Literary Messenger* said:

In all her extensive arrangements, there is not a single accommodation for religion.[62]

And here's what James Alexander wrote to John Hall after a visit to the university in 1847, when the religifying effort was well underway:

Jefferson knew how to select one of the finest plateaus in the land for this college. His antichristian plans have been singularly thwarted in every way.[63]

That's how Jefferson and the University of Virginia were written about from the time of the university's founding through 1840s.

By the late 1850s, however, most people who would have been old enough to remember Jefferson during his lifetime were dead, and the mythical, much less secular Jefferson could be born.

Not only was Henry Randall's biography of Jefferson written during this time when Jefferson's image was being *improved*, but Randall's obvious hero worship of Jefferson led his biography to be highly biased and at times quite inaccurate. The section of Randall's biography that Barton gets his University of Virginia information from is a good example of this problem.

Barton claims that John Holt Rice was a friend of the university, even though all of the primary sources – like Rice's own articles and Jefferson's letters about Rice – show that Rice was anything but a friend of the university. But this isn't new. Henry Randall, in his 1858 Jefferson biography, also claimed that Rice was a friend of the university. Randall didn't go to the primary source – Rice's own writings – either. Randall's source in *his* footnote for the claim that

---

62. "The University of Virginia," *Southern Literary Messenger,* Vol. VIII, Issue 1, January 1842, 54.

63. James W. Alexander to John Hall, May 27, 1847, John Hall, D.D., ed., *Forty Years' Familiar Letters of James W. Alexander, D.D.*, vol. 2, (New York: Charles Scribner, 1860), 71.

Rice was a friend of the university was the editorial comments in an 1856 book of letters between Jefferson and Joseph Cabell titled *Early history of the University of Virginia: As contained in the letters of Thomas Jefferson and Joseph C. Cabell.*

Randall actually says in his footnote that he did not even see John Holt Rice's 1818 or 1820 articles, but relied entirely on what the editor of the book of Jefferson-Cabell letters said for his opinion of Rice. Here's what Randall said in his footnote for his claim about Rice:

> We have not seen his articles, but the apparently candid editor of the History of the University describes him as a courteous and liberal man, a non-combatant in politics, a zealous advocate of education, and a known friend of the University.[64]

The problem here, besides the fact that Randall admittedly never even looked at what Rice himself actually wrote, is that the editor of this book of Jefferson-Cabell letters really can't be relied on as a "candid" source on the subject of John Holt Rice. The editor, Nathaniel Francis Cabell, was one of the many members of the Cabell family who had strong ties to Hampden-Sydney College, and was actually a student there when John Holt Rice was the professor of the college's theological seminary (the one that the Presbyterians were establishing in 1822 that made it unlikely that they would take Jefferson up on his invitation to establish a school near the university). Henry Stephens Randall just took the word of Nathaniel Francis Cabell that Rice was a friend of the university, and didn't even bother reading what Rice himself actually wrote.

Now, since Henry Stephens Randall admittedly didn't read Rice's articles on the university, we might be able to give him the benefit of the doubt and just chalk it up to sloppy research that he didn't know what Rice had done. But, we can't give that same benefit of the doubt to David Barton, since he definitely *did* read at

---

64. Henry S. Randall, *The Life of Thomas Jefferson*, vol. 3, (New York, Derby & Jackson, 1858), 466n.

least one of Rice's articles – the one from 1818 in the previous section that he deliberately quoted out of context.

This next example of how Jefferson was written about prior to the 1850s is a good one to read at this point because, in addition to being a typical example of the attitude towards Jefferson from the 1830s, it happens to be a book review of a biography of Jefferson written about twenty years before Randall's. The author of this Jefferson biography, written in 1837, was George Tucker. Tucker, of course, was the same original University of Virginia professor whose statement about the religions of the university's original professors was solicited by Randall for his 1858 Jefferson biography, and then edited a bit by Barton for *The Jefferson Lies*.

This book review of Tucker's *The Life of Thomas Jefferson, Third President of the United States,* appeared in the March 1837 issue of the *New-York Review and Quarterly Church Journal*. It was a lengthy review, with even the section on the university alone being quite long, but I'm including that section here in its entirety because it should be read in its entirety. This was how the *real* Thomas Jefferson was written about in 1837, just over a decade after his death:

A word now as to his proselyting spirit. The favorite project of Mr. Jefferson's latter days, was, as is well known, the establishment, in his native state, of a literary institution, which should surpass any of the higher seminaries of learning on this continent; and attaining deservedly to the name and character of an *University,* should attract students from all parts of the land. In this cause he labored with a perseverance which the weight of increasing years was not able to destroy. The accomplishment of this object he was prepared to enrol among the most important achievements of his long and busy life; and among what he deemed the splendid trophies to his fame, which he was desirous should perpetuate his memory to posterity, he placed his agency in the creation of the University of Virginia: he ordered it to be inscribed upon the marble which covers his remains, that he was the "FATHER" of this institution. And his zeal in its behalf was of no sudden growth, for while the subject of founding the University was yet before the leg-islature, he requests a confidential correspondent to inform him of its progress and fate, and thus proceeds:

"I have only this single anxiety in the world. It is a bantling of forty years' birth and nursing; and if I can once see it on its legs, I will sing with sincerity and pleasure my *nunc dimitlas.*"

And now what was, in Mr. Jefferson's purpose, to be the character of this bantling, nursed so long and with such affectionate solici-tude? Let Mr. Jefferson himself answer. In a letter to William Short, from which we have already quoted, he thus speaks: —

"The history of our University you know so far. Seven of the ten pavilions destined for the professors, and about thirty dormitories, will be completed this year, and three others, with six hotels for boarding, and seventy other dormitories, will be completed the next year, and the whole be in readiness then to receive those who are to occupy them. But means to bring these into place, and to set the machine into motion, must come from the legislature. An opposition, in the mean time, has been got up. That of our alma mater, William and Mary, is not of much weight. She must descend into the secondary rank of academies of preparation for the Univer-sity. The serious enemies are the priests of the different religious sects, to whose spells on the human mind, its improvement is ominous. Their pulpits are now resounding with denunciations against the appointment of Doctor Cooper, whom they charge as a monotheist in opposition to their tritheism. Hostile as these sects are, in every other point, to one another, they unite in maintaining their mystical theogony against those who believe there is one God only. The Presbyterian clergy are loudest; the most intolerant of all sects, the most tyrannical and ambitious; ready at the word of the lawgiver, if such a word could be now obtained, to put the torch to the pile, and to rekindle in this virgin hemisphere the flames in which their oracle Calvin consumed the poor Servetus, because he could not find in his Euclid the proposition which has demonstrated that three are one, and one is three, nor subscribe to that of Calvin, that magistrates have a right to exterminate all heretics to the Calvinistic creed. They pant to re-establish, *by law,* that holy inquisition, which they can now only infuse into *public opinion.* We have most unwisely committed to the hierophants of our particular superstition the direction of public opinion, that lord of the universe. We have given them stated and privileged days to collect and catechize us, opportunities of delivering their oracles to the people in mass, and of moulding their minds as wax in the hollow of their hands. But in despite of their fulminations against endeavors to enlighten the general mind, to improve the reason of the people, and encourage them in the use of it, the liberality of this State will support this institution, and give fair play to the cultivation of reason. Can you ever find a more eligible occasion of visiting once more your native country, than that of accompanying Mr. Correa, and of seeing with him this beautiful and hopeful institution *in ovo?"*

It seems then that this mighty travail of forty years was to give to the youth of the United States an institution, made permanent by rich endowments, and cherished by national pride, in which they were to be taught, at least so far as Mr. Jefferson's influence could extend itself for that purpose, that "the priests of the different religious sects" were imposing "spells on the human mind:" – that the clergy of one of the most numerous and respectable denominations in the United States were panting to exercise a bloody tyranny over the souls and bodies of their fellow citizens; that the religion of Christ professed by so many of our countrymen was a "particular superstition;" that to "the hierophants" of that superstition, alias, the public teachers of Christianity, no opportunity should be afforded of addressing themselves to their fellow-beings on the subject of their immortal interests; that "stated and privileged days" on which to collect the people for this purpose should not be set apart and consecrated to this end, that is, that the Sabbath should be abolished; that God Almighty was not the "Lord of the Universe," for that most vague, and uncertain and fluctuating of all things changeable, viz. *public opinion* was the rightful heir to the throne of heaven; and that "this beautiful and hopeful institution," fostered and supported by the liberality of the State, would carry out these principles, would persevere in these noble "endeavors to enlighten the general mind, to improve the reason of the people, and encourage them in the use of it," in other words, would lend its powerful aid to the maintenance of a refined and civilized heathenism. This was the bantling which was forty years in coming to the birth, this was the "beautiful and hopeful" offspring which was to reflect deathless honor on its paternity; and the dealing parent only wished to see this interesting child of his affections able to stand upon its legs, when he would be ready to sing his *nunc dimittas,* and lie down in the grave comforted by the sweet consciousness, that he had sowed the seed which would yield a plentiful harvest of posthumous mischief! Verily "the hierophants" of the "particular superstition" are here thrown into the distance; never in the exercise of their most artful cunning did they devise a machine as mighty for the work of proselyting. This was indeed a plan for poisoning the stream at the fountain. Ardent, generous, gifted and unsuspecting youth, was here made the victim of a deliberate, cold-blooded, calculating design for its corruption. An attempt was here systematically made to undermine that which, whether true or false, was giving comfort to thousands, affording stability to virtue, and the existence of which wrought no practical injury to Mr. Jefferson; for he was in the full enjoyment of every right, natural and civil, and no human power could molest him.

The University was opened, and as is well known, all religious instruction was excluded: *the experiment failed;* and the professors and students themselves resorted to the plan which is now pursued of employing a chaplain. Professor Tucker informs us too that while Mr. Jefferson was yet alive, and before a chaplain was provided, he was in the habit of having some of the students as invited guests at his table on every Sunday; and we happen to know that on such occasions, Christianity was frequently made the subject of his conversation and his sneers. The truth is, whether Mr. Jefferson was aware of it or not, that he entertained a hatred of Christianity, as commonly understood and received, more intensely virulent than all the hostility which he represents as being so abundant and merciless between the different denominations of Christians; and in the indulgence of that hatred he was ready enough to make proselytes to his opinions.[65]

Reading this 1837 opinion of Jefferson and the other examples in this book of how Jefferson was written about during his lifetime and in the several decades that followed, how could anyone possibly believe the main premise of David Barton's *The Jefferson Lies* – his claim that modern academics and secularists are revising history? What was written about Jefferson and the University of Virginia in the 1820s, 1830s, and 1840s not only confirms that what Barton claims is modern revisionism is not revisionism at all, but what was written about Jefferson prior to the 1850s often went even further than most modern academics go.

The 1837 review of Tucker's biography of Jefferson touches on many points, the most important of which we'll get to in the next section, but first there are a few more lies from Barton's answer to his question "Was Jefferson's faculty composed of Unitarians?" that we need to knock off.

---

65. "Character of Jefferson," *The New-York Review and Quarterly Church Journal,* Vol. 1, No. 1, March 1837, 17-19.

The One About
Jefferson and Thomas Cooper

BARTON'S LIE: Jefferson withdrew the University of Virginia's offer to Dr. Thomas Cooper to be a professor because it became known that he was a Unitarian and there was a public outcry.

THE TRUTH: The university never withdrew its offer to Thomas Cooper. He resigned to accept the presidency of South Carolina College due to delays in the opening of the University of Virginia.

It's not until this section of his book, the section on Jefferson's not hiring Unitarians as professors, that Barton finally gets around to mentioning Dr. Thomas Cooper. Cooper, of course, was the Unitarian professor whose hiring by Jefferson provided the fodder for John Holt Rice's attack on the university in 1820. But Barton doesn't mention Cooper earlier when writing about John Holt Rice because Cooper doesn't fit into his revisionist story about John Holt Rice's being a friend of the university. According to Barton:

> "...Jefferson once invited Thomas Cooper to be professor of chemistry and law, but when it became known that Cooper was a Unitarian, a public outcry arose against him and Jefferson and the university withdrew its offer to him.

We've already gone through enough of the Thomas Cooper story in the last section to know that the public outcry that "arose against him" was the result of John Holt Rice's alarmist articles claiming that Jefferson was hiring only Unitarians and founding a "deistical" or "atheistical" university. And we also know that Jefferson didn't merely "invite" Cooper to be a professor. This wasn't some fleeting and easily dismissed thought that Jefferson had, as Barton's choice of words implies. The Board of Visitors had actually entered into a contract with Cooper in 1817, when the university was still Central College, and still intended for him to be a professor even after Rice began his attack and "a public outcry arose against him" in 1820.

Barton's claim that the university withdrew its offer to Cooper is simply not true. The source that Barton cites for this claim does not say that the university withdrew its offer. It says that the university was going to renegotiate its contract with Cooper. This was not because of Cooper's being a Unitarian or the trouble started by Rice. It was because of the uncertainty about when the university would be able to open and a lack of funds to pay Cooper what he was promised he'd be paid while waiting for the university to open. Cooper had been under contract since 1817. As of 1820, it was still uncertain when the university would actually be able to open, but it was clear at that point that was likely to be several more years.

If you look up Barton's source for his claim, what you find is a resolution of the Board of Visitors, passed in April 1820 – almost a year before Cooper informed Jefferson that he decided to stay at South Carolina College and was resigning from the university.

> Resolved, that the committee of superintendence be authorized to communicate to Doctor Thomas Cooper the delay and uncertainty now unavoidable in regard to the time of opening the University, and to make such change in the contracts with him as to them may seem advisable.[66]

---

66. Albert Ellery Bergh, ed., *The Writings of Thomas Jefferson*, vol. 19, (Washington D.C.: Thomas Jefferson Memorial Association, 1907), 389.

The committee appointed at the Board of Visitors' April 1820 meeting to contact Dr. Cooper to renegotiate his contract consisted of Jefferson and John Hartwell Cocke. According to his contract at that time, Cooper was to be paid a salary of $1,500 while waiting for the university to open, but the board didn't have the funds to pay him.

What needs to be understood here is that Thomas Cooper wasn't just any professor. He was a big name who would attract students to the university. Jefferson had been trying to get him since 1814, even before Central College, when his plan for a university was still in its earliest stages and called Albemarle Academy. The Board of Visitors was actually paying this guy to wait to make sure it was their university that got him. Barton's minimization of Cooper by referring to him as merely someone whom "Jefferson once invited ... to be professor" is thoroughly inaccurate.

At its March 1819 meeting, the board's first official meeting as the Board of Visitors of the University of Virginia, the appointment of Cooper as a professor and the contract Central College had made with him in 1817 were confirmed. These were the terms of Cooper's contract from that March 1819 board meeting:

> ... in addition to his permanent salary of 1,500 dollars he shall receive such sums during the first and second years as, with his salary and his tuition fees, shall amount, in the whole, to not less than 3,500 dollars a year, to commence on the first Monday of April of the ensuing year, 1820, or so soon after as he shall arrive at the University.[67]

As you can see from this, as of March 1819 the board was expecting the university to open in April 1820, meaning that at this point they were only expecting to have to compensate Cooper for one more year of waiting for the university to open. They expected him to be at the university teaching by April 1820. But, obviously, things

---

67. Albert Ellery Bergh, ed., *The Writings of Thomas Jefferson*, vol. 19, (Washington D.C.: Thomas Jefferson Memorial Association, 1907), 377.

didn't work out as expected. The university was not ready to open in April 1820. So, at the April 1820 meeting of the Board of Visitors, the committee of Jefferson and Cocke was appointed to renegotiate with Cooper.

Although the April 1820 decision to renegotiate Cooper's contract was due to the uncertainty over when the university would open and the lack of funds to pay him while he was waiting, it was also three months after John Holt Rice launched his attack and got the clergy and a large part of the public calling for Cooper to be removed. This led a few of the board members, including Cocke, to see the university's financial situation as a possible way out of the problem caused by John Holt Rice. But, Cooper had a contract, and terminating that contract had to be a mutual decision.

Just to remove any possible doubt that it was the university's delay in opening and finances – and not Rice's attack – that led to the decision to renegotiate Cooper's contract, the board had already decided that Cooper's contract needed to be renegotiated at its October 1819 meeting, three months *before* Rice's January 1820 article came out. From the October 1819 board meeting:

> It appearing to the Board that the buildings and the funds of the University will not be in a condition to justify the commencement of any of its schools during the next spring, and that, therefore, the duties of the professorships to which Dr. Thomas Cooper was appointed must be deferred, the committee of superintendence is instructed to communicate that fact to Dr. Cooper, to arrange with him the terms on which the delay may be made, consistent with his convenience, and conformable to an honorable fulfillment of our engagements with him; and to report their proceedings to the Board at their next meeting.[68]

Now, if you remember from the previous section, when Cooper first found out about John Holt Rice's January 1820 attack on him,

---

68. Albert Ellery Bergh, ed., *The Writings of Thomas Jefferson*, vol. 19, (Washington D.C.: Thomas Jefferson Memorial Association, 1907), 381.

he actually wrote to Jefferson offering to resign if Jefferson thought he should. That was weeks before the April 1820 board meeting, so Jefferson knew at that meeting that Cooper would resign if he asked him to. But Jefferson didn't want Cooper to resign, so he didn't let the rest of the board know at that meeting that Cooper had already offered to resign. Jefferson wanted to find a way that the university could release Cooper from his contract but rehire him when the university eventually did open, so, before doing anything official, he wanted to write to Cooper unofficially.

Unlike James Madison and the majority of the other board members who were with Jefferson in wanting to do everything possible to keep Cooper, Jefferson's fellow committee member, John Hartwell Cocke, was one of the few board members who were wavering and starting to think that however big an asset Cooper would be to the university, he might not be worth the trouble he was causing with the clergy and the public. Cocke was also the one board member who, for his own personal religious reasons, did seem to have a problem with Cooper's being a Unitarian. Nevertheless, he agreed to let Jefferson write to Cooper. (In reality, Jefferson always got his way, but he did still consult the other board members to get their approval before acting – at least most of the time.)

Cooper, like Jefferson, didn't want to close the door on any future possibilities once the university opened, and didn't technically resign his appointment as a professor. After being contacted by Jefferson, he simply said that the $1,500 promised in his original contract would be sufficient to cover his losses and expenses, letting the university out of the contract under which they would have had to continue paying him.

That Jefferson had no intention of letting Cooper go is clear from their correspondence over the next year. The following, for example, is what Jefferson wrote to Cooper four months later.

> In the consultations of the Visitors of the University on the subject of releasing you from your engagement with us, although one or two members seemed alarmed at this cry of fire from the Presbyterian pulpits, yet the real ground of

our decision was that our funds were in fact hypotheti-
cated for five or six years to redeem the loan we had
reluctantly made; and although we hoped and trusted
that the ensuing legislature would remit the debt and lib-
erate our funds, yet it was not just, on this possibility, to
stand in the way of your looking out for a more certain
provision. ...

The legislature meets on the 1st Monday of December,
and before Christmas we shall know what are their intentions. If such as we expect, we shall then immediately
take measures to engage our professors and bring them
into place the ensuing autumn or early winter. My hope is
that you will be able and willing to keep yourself uncom-
mitted, to take your place among them about that time;
and I can assure you there is not a voice among us which
will not be cordially given for it. I think, too, I may add, that
if the Presbyterian opposition should not die by that time,
it will be directed at once against the whole institution,
and not amuse itself with nibbling at a single object. It did
that only because there was no other, and they might
think it politic to mask their designs on the body of the
fortress, under the [feint] of a battery against a single
bastion. I will not despair then of the avail of your services
in an establishment which I contemplate as the future
bulwark of the human mind in this hemisphere. [69]

It wasn't until March of 1821 that Dr. Cooper informed Jefferson
and Madison that he had accepted a permanent position at South
Carolina College. Although Jefferson had done his best to assure
Cooper that the clergy's attacks against him would die down and
that the Board of Visitors would be behind him, the trustees of

---

69. Thomas Jefferson to Dr. Thomas Cooper, August 14, 1820. Albert Ellery Bergh, ed.,
The Writings of Thomas Jefferson, vol. 15, (Washington D.C.: Thomas Jefferson Memorial
Association, 1903), 267-269.

South Carolina College had already unanimously pushed for the legislature of that state to increase his salary, and had elected him president of the college. Cooper, whose family had been waiting in Philadelphia this entire time because they weren't sure whether they should move to Virginia or South Carolina, couldn't pass up this guaranteed position, particularly after finding out on a visit to Jefferson a few months earlier that the opening date of the university was still as uncertain as ever.

A decade later, Cooper was attacked by the Presbyterian clergy of South Carolina, but the legislature exonerated him of all the clergy's accusations and, although stepping down as president, he remained at South Carolina College as a professor until 1834.

There is no truth whatsoever to David Barton's claim that the University of Virginia withdrew its offer to Thomas Cooper because it became known that he was a Unitarian. The letters of Jefferson, Cooper, and other university board members, as well as the minutes of the university's board meetings, all show that the decision to resign was Cooper's, and that this had nothing to do with the religious attacks against him or the outcry over his Unitarianism.

The One About
Jefferson and Unitarian Professors

As I said at the beginning of this section, Barton's question – "Was Jefferson's Faculty Composed of Unitarians?" – is a straw man. There really were no Unitarians among the original professors at the university, and nobody but that obscure writer who Barton found to quote would say anything different. But this absence of Unitarians on the university's faculty says nothing whatsoever about Jefferson.

The question that should be asked is: "Did Jefferson *want* a faculty composed of Unitarians?" The answer to that question would seem to be yes.

Had it not been for the attack by John Holt Rice on Thomas Cooper, Jefferson would have been free to pursue other Unitarian professors. Cooper himself might or might not have ended up on the faculty. Although the reasons that Cooper ended up at South Carolina College rather than the university were the delays in the university's opening and its finances, the attacks by the clergy played a role in causing the delays in the legislature that were partially responsible for the hold-ups and financial problems. In any event, there is absolutely no doubt that Jefferson *wanted* the Unitarian Cooper on the faculty more than any other professor.

Then there were George Ticknor and Nathaniel Bowditch, both of whom were Unitarians. As I wrote in a previous section, the university's Board of Visitors, at their October 1820 meeting, passed a resolution to begin negotiations with Ticknor, who was then a professor at Harvard, a school that had been under Unitarian control since 1805, and Bowditch, who was a member of a Unitarian church in Massachusetts. Any hope of bringing one or both of these Unitarian professors to the university was dashed, however, when Joseph Cabell found out from his 1822 meeting with John Holt Rice that the religious opinions of Ticknor and Bowditch had already been investigated by the Presbyterians. At this point, it was apparent that the Presbyterians were going to subject every candidate for a professorship at the university to an anti-Unitarian religious test. Jefferson no longer had a choice. He couldn't even try to hire any Unitarians.

Nothing changes the fact that Jefferson *wanted* to hire three Unitarians that we know of, and quite possibly would have hired others, if the trinitarian clergy hadn't made it impossible for him to hire any Unitarians. Therefore, the fact that there were no Unitarians on Jefferson's faculty doesn't mean diddly-squat.

Furthermore, there was actually a fourth Unitarian who Jefferson said he would have liked to have had at the university who I probably wouldn't even have thought of while writing this if it weren't for checking the footnote for Barton's next misquote.

The One About
Jefferson and a Unitarian Nobody's Ever Heard Of

Barton concludes his section on the absence of Unitarians on the faculty of the University of Virginia with this:

> Obviously, this type of original primary-source evidence concerning Jefferson and the religious views of his faculty is ignored by many of today's writers. But Professor Roy Honeywell of Eastern Michigan University was a professor from a much earlier period who actually did review the original historical evidence. He correctly concluded:
>
> > In general, Jefferson seems to have ignored the religious affiliations of the professors. His objection to ministers was because of their active association with sectarian groups, in his day a fruitful source of social friction. The charge that he intended the University to be a center of Unitarian influence is totally groundless.

Barton chops off the end of Professor Roy Honeywell's last sentence here, but more importantly he omits the letter written by Jefferson that Honeywell used to support the part of his sentence that Barton chops off.

Professor Honeywell, writing in that "much earlier period" of 1931, presents the expected not-so-secular version of Jefferson typical of books written after the 1850s, where Jefferson's dislike of the clergy is toned down and he merely had a "friendly attitude" towards Unitarianism. But then, contradicting himself, he quoted a letter in which Jefferson not only came right out and said that he was a Unitarian, but said that he wished he could bring a Unitarian minister to the university not just to teach but to preach.

But it's not this 1930s professor's spin on things that matters here; it's that Barton selectively quotes what Honeywell wrote, completely disregarding what Jefferson said in the letter that Honeywell quoted – ironically ignoring this "original primary-source evidence" right after touting Honeywell as someone who reviewed the "original primary-source evidence."

Here's what Professor Honeywell wrote, complete with the part chopped off by Barton (in bold), and the letter that Barton ignores:

> In general, Jefferson seems to have ignored the religious affiliations of the professors. His objection to ministers was because of their active association with sectarian groups, in his day a fruitful source of social friction. The charge that he intended the University to be a center of Unitarian influence is totally groundless, **though his friendly attitude toward the tenets of that sect is shown in his letter of January 8, 1825, to Benjamin Waterhouse:**

> > Your favor of Dec. 24 is received, the Professors of our University, 8 in number are all engaged, those of ant. and Mod. lang. are already on the spot. 3 more are hourly expected to arrive, and on their arrival the whole will assemble & enter on their duties, there remains therefore no place in which we can avail ourselves of the services of the rev'd mr. Bertrum as a teacher. I wish we could do it as a Preacher. I am anxious to see the doctrine of one god commenced in our state. But the popul'n of my neighb'hood is too slender, and is too much divided into other sects to maintain any one preacher well. I must

therefore be contented to be an Unitarian by myself, although I know there are many around me who would become so, if once they could hear the questions fairly stated.[70]

What part of Jefferson's saying "I must therefore be contented to be an Unitarian by myself" is open to interpretation? The man said he was a Unitarian.

And George Tucker, who was at the University of Virginia when it opened, and is obviously considered a reliable source by Barton, who quotes him regarding the religious beliefs of the professors, wrote in his 1837 biography of Jefferson:

In the last years of his life, when questioned by any of his friends on this subject, he used to say he was "an Unitarian."[71]

And what about Jefferson's saying in his letter to Benjamin Waterhouse that he wished he could bring the Unitarian Rev. Bertrum to the university as a preacher? Were John Holt Rice and the other trinitarian clergy right when they accused Jefferson of wanting to promote Unitarianism at his university?

As quoted earlier, the author of the book review of George Tucker's biography of Jefferson in the *New-York Review and Quarterly Church Journal* wrote in 1837 that the university's intent was:

... to give to the youth of the United States an institution, made permanent by rich endowments, and cherished by national pride, in which they were to be taught, at least so far as Mr. Jefferson's influence could extend itself for that purpose, that "the priests of the different religious sects" were imposing "spells on the human mind."

70. Roy J. Honeywell, *The Educational Work of Thomas Jefferson*, (Cambridge: Harvard University Press, 1931), 92.
71. George Tucker, *The Life of Thomas Jefferson, Third President of the United States*, vol. 2, (London: Charles Knight and Co., 1837), 563.

Was the author of that 1837 review right? Did Jefferson really intend to use the university to steer students away from trinitarian Christianity and towards Unitarianism? He certainly did made it crystal clear in numerous letters to Benjamin Waterhouse, Thomas Cooper, William Short, and other Unitarian friends that he wanted Unitarianism to spread.

As we'll see in the next section, in April 1825, just three months after writing to Benjamin Waterhouse that he wished he could bring a Unitarian minister to the university as a preacher, Jefferson denied a request from a member of the university's staff to allow ministers of the various trinitarian sects to hold worship services on the campus on Sundays.

3. Did Jefferson Bar Religious Instruction from the Academic Program?

As the reviewer of George Tucker's biography of Jefferson wrote in the *New-York Review and Quarterly Church Journal* in 1837, "The University was opened, and as is well known, all religious instruction was excluded." And this *was* well know in the 1820s, 1830s, and 1840s. It only became less well known as the authors of the latter part of the 1800s began to *improve* Jefferson's image, so that now someone like David Barton can get away with claiming that what was a well-known fact in Jefferson's lifetime and the decades that followed isn't true.

Barton begins this section of *The Jefferson Lies*:

In 1818 Jefferson and the university Visitors publicly released their plan for the new school. In addition to announcing that it would be transdenominational and that religious instruction would be provided to all students, Jefferson took further intentional steps to ensure that religious training would occur.

The only true statement in Barton's opening paragraph for this section is the first sentence: "In 1818 Jefferson and the university Visitors publicly released their plan for the new school." They did not announce that the university would be "transdenominational" or that religious instruction would be provided to all students, and Jefferson most certainly did not take any "intentional steps to ensure that religious training would occur."

What Barton relies on for several of his claims in this section is the *Rockfish Report*. As explained in an earlier section, this was the 1818 report written by Jefferson to get the legislature to choose Central College as the state university. It was in this report that Jefferson dropped the bombshell that his university would have no professor of divinity. To diffuse this bombshell, he threw in a few things to give the impression that the school would still provide some kind of religious instruction, even if it didn't have a divinity professor. As also explained earlier, Jefferson had no intention of there being any religious instruction at the university when he wrote this 1818 report, as his actions once the legislature officially named Central College as the University of Virginia clearly show.

The things that Barton claims as proof that Jefferson included religious instruction at the university never happened. These things were merely put into the *Rockfish Report* to get over the hurdle of getting the legislature to approve the university. Once that hurdle was cleared, Jefferson simply disregarded them.

We've already gone over one example of this – that the *Rockfish Report* said the university's ethics professor was going to be teaching religion, but when it came time to actually hire what was supposed to be an ethics professor, Jefferson and Madison (being limited to ten professors) clearly wanted to use the ethics professor slot for something they considered more important. The two candidates proposed by Jefferson were both lawyers, and Madison proposed George Tucker, whose primary field was economics. As Jefferson wrote to Madison in the letter quoted in the earlier section on this, any professor who was worthy of a spot on the faculty to teach some other subject would be capable of throwing in some moral philosophy and ethics, saying that ethics was even "more trite" than "the general science of the mind," which he said was "a branch of science of little difficulty to any ingenious man." Jefferson's so-called "ethics" professor wasn't even really going to be an ethics professor, let alone an ethics professor who was going to be teaching religion. Jefferson completely ignored what he said in the *Rockfish Report* and used the ethics slot to hire an economics professor who could also teach a few other subjects that had nothing to do with religion. Since Tucker's experience, in addition to his work in economics, included being a politician and a writer, rhetoric and *belles lettres* (literature) were the other subjects assigned to him.

In this section, Barton not only keeps up his lie about the ethics professor teaching religion, but adds a few bigger lies to it.

The One About
Jefferson and Ancient Languages

BARTON'S LIE: Jefferson made religion part of the study of ancient languages at the university.

THE TRUTH: Jefferson had no religious reason for teaching ancient languages at the university.

Here's Barton's claim about Jefferson's making religious instruction a reason for teaching ancient languages:

> ... he directed the professor of ancient languages to teach Biblical Greek, Hebrew, and Latin to students so that they would be equipped to study the "earliest and most respected authorities of the faith of every sect [denomination].

Barton adds the word "Biblical" to describe these languages, although the word "Biblical" is nowhere in the *Rockfish Report*. Neither is the quote that Barton uses as the reason these languages would be taught.

At the end of the paragraph in the *Rockfish Report* in which Jefferson dropped the bombshell that there would be no professor of divinity, but quickly said that the ethics professor would be teaching some religion, he tagged on a line implying that the teaching of ancient languages had a religious purpose. Here's the whole paragraph from the Rockfish Report:

> In conformity with the principles of our Constitution, which places all sects of religion on an equal footing, with the jealousies of the different sects in guarding that equality from encroachment and surprise, and with the sentiments of the Legislature in favor of freedom of religion, manifested on former occasions, we have proposed no professor of divinity; and the rather as the proofs of the being of a God, the creator, preserver, and supreme ruler of the universe, the author of all the relations of morality, and of the laws and obligations these infer, will be within the province of the professor of ethics; to which adding the developments of these moral obligations, of those in which all sects agree, with a knowledge of the languages, Hebrew, Greek, and Latin, a basis will be formed common to all sects. Proceeding thus far without offence to the Constitution, we have thought it proper at this point to leave every sect to provide, as they think fittest, the means of further instruction in their own peculiar tenets.[72]

Jefferson really didn't want a professorship of ancient languages at the university at all, for the same reason he wanted to get rid of the professorship of Greek and Latin at William and Mary in 1779. He thought that teaching Greek and Latin, which he thought university students should already be proficient in, would attract students who were too young. This is also from the *Rockfish Report*:

> A professor is proposed for ancient languages, the Latin, Greek, and Hebrew, particularly; but these languages being the foundation common to all the sciences, it is difficult to foresee what may be the extent of this school. At the same time, no greater obstruction to industrious study could be proposed than the presence, the

---

72. *Early History of the University of Virginia, as Contained in the Letters of Thomas Jefferson and Joseph C. Cabell*, (Richmond, VA: J.W. Randolph, 1856), 441-442.

intrusions and the noisy turbulence of a multitude of small boys; and if they are to be placed here for the rudiments of the languages, they may be so numerous that its character and value as an University will be merged in those of a Grammar school. It is, therefore, greatly to be wished, that preliminary schools, either on private or public establishment, could be distributed in districts through the State, as preparatory to the entrance of students into the University.[73]

Did Jefferson really consider Hebrew to be among the languages that he considered "the foundation common to all the sciences" when he lumped it in with Greek and Latin in the *Rockfish Report*? Apparently not, since it was dropped when the university actually opened, right along with that religious instruction the ethics professor was going to be teaching.

Hebrew was not taught at the university, and the reason for teaching Greek and Latin was not that they were "Biblical" languages, as Barton implies by quoting something that isn't from the *Rockfish Report*. What Barton quotes is from 1822, when Jefferson was trying to stop the clergy's attacks on the university by inviting the religious sects to open their own theological schools near the university. In the Board of Visitors' October 1822 report to the legislature, the report in which the invitation to the religious sects was extended, Jefferson made the most of the ancient languages thing, writing that the *Rockfish Report* had provided for:

... giving instruction in the Hebrew, Greek and Latin languages, the depositories of the originals, and of the earliest and most respected authorities of the faith of every sect ...[74]

Jefferson's reason for teaching Greek and Latin was always that these languages were "the foundation common to all the sciences." The fact that these were the same languages of early religious writ-

73. *Early History of the University of Virginia, as Contained in the Letters of Thomas Jefferson and Joseph C. Cabell*, (Richmond, VA: J.W. Randolph, 1856), 438-439.
74. Ibid., 474.

ings was just convenient and useful when Jefferson wanted to make it sound like the university wasn't excluding religion. And, as I said, Hebrew was dropped when the university actually opened and the pretense that there would be some kind of religious instruction there no longer had to be kept up.

Barton ends his paragraph about "Biblical" languages being taught for the purpose of reading early religious writings by saying that Jefferson "wanted the writings of prominent Christian authorities to be placed in the university library," and that he asked James Madison to "prepare a list of Christian theological writings" for the library.

Of course Jefferson included books on religion in the university library, and he did ask Madison to compile a list. Jefferson wouldn't have considered any library complete without a religion section. But he also didn't consider a religion section complete without books on religions *other than* Christianity, as well as books disputing Christian doctrines. Barton's claim that Jefferson asked Madison specifically for "Christian theological writings" is a lie.

Here's what Jefferson wrote to Madison while working on the catalog for the library, after having already made a list himself of the good "Christian, as well as Pagan" moral writers:

> It has been laborious far beyond my expectation, having already devoted 4. hours a day to it for upwards of two months, and the whole day for some time past and not yet in sight of the end. It will enable us to judge what the object will cost. The chapter in which I am most at a loss is that of divinity; and knowing that in your early days you bestowed attention on this subject, I wish you could suggest to me any works really worthy of a place in the catalogue. The good moral writers, Christian as well as Pagan I have set down; but there are writers of celebrity in religious metaphysics, such as Duns Scotus etc. alii tales [and others of such kind] whom you can suggest.[75]

75. Jefferson to James Madison, August 8, 1824. James Morton Smith, ed., *The Republic of Letters: The Correspondence Between Thomas Jefferson and James Madison 1776-1826*, vol. 3, (New York and London: W.W. Norton & Company, 1995), 1897.

Jefferson apparently overestimated Madison's knowledge of the subject, as Madison noted in his reply:

> I will endeavor to make out a list of Theological Works, but am less qualified for the task than you seem to think ...[76]

For two guys who were supposedly so religious and so well versed in theological works, they certainly seem to have been having a hard time with this task, don't they?

After receiving a letter from Jefferson a few weeks later asking him to hurry up and finish the list, Madison realized that Jefferson hadn't meant for him to compile anything nearly as extensive as what he had started working on. But Madison did send Jefferson what he had already put together by that point. That's where Barton gets the bunch of early Christian writers that he rattles off in his next paragraph. For one of his sentences, Barton just copies a string of Christian names from the "Miscellaneous" section of Madison's list and doesn't mention that Madison also had the Koran in that same section, as well as Unitarian writers like Joseph Priestley. And of course he completely disregards that Jefferson had told Madison that he had already made the list of "Pagan" writers. According to Barton, Jefferson only wanted "Christian theological writings" in the university library.

Barton's next lie is also about a library catalog, although his readers wouldn't know that since he claims that what he's quoting was about something else entirely.

---

76. Jefferson to James Madison, August 8, 1824. James Morton Smith, ed., *The Republic of Letters: The Correspondence Between Thomas Jefferson and James Madison 1776-1826,* vol. 3, (New York and London: W.W. Norton & Company, 1995), 1898.

The One About
Jefferson Making Law and Political Science Religious

BARTON'S LIE: Jefferson made religion an "inseparable part" of law and political science education at the University of Virginia.

THE TRUTH: Religion was not a part of law and political science education at the university. Barton lies about a letter that had absolutely nothing to do with the curriculum of the university to make this claim.

According to Barton:

> In addition to religious instruction given by the professor of ethics and the professor of ancient languages, Jefferson personally ensured that religious study would also be an inseparable part of the study of law and political science as he explained to a prominent judge:
>
>> [I]n my catalogue, considering ethics, as well as religion as supplements to law in the government of man, I had placed them in that sequence."

What Barton quotes here is from a letter Jefferson wrote to

Augustus Woodward regarding the best arrangement for a library catalog. This letter had nothing to do with making "religious study ... an inseparable part of the study of law and political science" at the university."

Even Barton himself has said that this letter wasn't about the University of Virginia. In his previous book, *Original Intent,* Barton used this very same quote from this very same letter, but in that book he claimed it was about Jefferson's 1778 plan for public schools in Virginia.

But this letter wasn't about either Jefferson's 1778 plan for public schools *or* the curriculum at the University of Virginia. It was just one library catalog aficionado writing to another library catalog aficionado.

Augustus Woodward was one of the founders of the University of Michigan, as well as a territorial judge. Woodward shared Jefferson's interest in books and, through numerous visits to libraries in major cities and discussions with various scholars, had developed a system for classifying all of the branches of science. This was published in 1816 as *A System of Universal Science.* In the letter quoted by Barton, Jefferson, who had come up with a different system for cataloging his own library, was simply explaining to Woodward how he had arrived at what he thought was the proper place for books on religion.

> The naturalists, you know, distribute the history of nature into three kingdoms or departments: zoology, botany, mineralogy. Ideology or mind, however, occupies so much space in the field of science, that we might perhaps erect it into a fourth kingdom or department. But, inasmuch as it makes a part of the animal construction only, it would be more proper to subdivide zoology into physical and moral. The latter including ideology, ethics, and mental science generally, in my catalogue, considering ethics, as well as religion, as supplements to law in the government of man, I had placed them in that sequence. But certainly the faculty of thought belongs to

animal history, is an important portion of it, and should there find its place.[77]

This is what Barton turns into: "Jefferson personally ensured that religious study would also be an inseparable part of the study of law and political science" at the university.

77. Jefferson to Judge Augustus B. Woodward, March 24, 1824. Albert Ellery Bergh, ed., *The Writings of Thomas Jefferson,* vol. 16, (Washington D.C.: Thomas Jefferson Memorial Association, 1907), 19.

The One About
Jefferson and Religious Worship on Campus

BARTON'S LIE: Jefferson approved of and encouraged religious worship on the University of Virginia campus.

THE TRUTH: Jefferson did everything he could to prevent religious worship on the University of Virginia campus, even lying to be able to deny a request to use a university building for Sunday worship services.

Jefferson also approved of worship on campus acknowledging "that a building ... in the middle of the grounds may be called for in time in which may be rooms for religious worship." He later ordered that in the university Rotunda, "one of its large elliptical rooms on its middle floor shall be used for... religious worship." He further declared that "the students of the University will be free and *expected* to attend religious worship at the establishment of their respective sect" (emphasis added).

The last sentence of Barton's paragraph is, of course, the same lie he used in the earlier section about Jefferson's invitation to the religious sects to establish their own schools near the university. In this section, Barton is still claiming that Jefferson "expected" university students to attend religious worship at religious schools that didn't exist. In Barton's repeat of this lie, Jefferson even "declared" that students would attend those nonexistent schools.

As for the rest of what Barton claims, the first quote he uses – "that a building ... in the middle of the grounds may be called for in time in which may be rooms for religious worship" – comes from the 1818 *Rockfish Report,* and the second quote is from the university rules, which were written at the October 1824 meeting of the Board of Visitors.

Both of these quotes were about the various purposes the rooms in the university's Rotunda might be used for (in the 1818 *Rockfish Report*), and could be used for (in the 1824 university rules).

This is the full quote from the *Rockfish Report,* found at the end of a section describing and estimating the cost of the buildings that had to be finished before the university could open:

> It is supposed probable, that a building of somewhat more size in the middle of the grounds may be called for in time, in which may be rooms for religious worship, under such impartial regulations as the Visitors shall prescribe, for public examinations, for a library, for the schools of music, drawing, and other associated purposes.[78]

The full quote from the 1824 rules, which Barton reduces to "one of its large elliptical rooms on its middle floor shall be used for... religious worship," was:

> One of its larger elliptical rooms on its middle floor shall be used for annual examinations, for lectures to such schools as are too numerous for their ordinary school room, and for religious worship, under the regulations allowed to be prescribed by law.[79]

---

78. *Early History of the University of Virginia, as Contained in the Letters of Thomas Jefferson and Joseph C. Cabell,* (Richmond, VA: J.W. Randolph, 1856), 434.

79. Albert Ellery Bergh, ed., *The Writings of Thomas Jefferson,* vol. 19, (Washington D.C.: Thomas Jefferson Memorial Association, 1907), 449-450.

Ironically, as we'll see in the next section, that statement in the university's 1824 rules that Barton edits to make it seem like Jefferson went out of his way to encourage religion by ordering that a large room in the Rotunda be used for religious worship was one of the things used by the clergy of the 1840s to prove that Jefferson tried to *prevent* religious worship by inconveniently making a multi-purpose room the only place on campus that religious worship could be held. Barton takes the very same rule that the clergy of the 1840s complained about, edits out all the other purposes that this room was used for, and uses his edited quote to claim that Jefferson devoted a large room to religious worship.

But it was the lengths that Jefferson went to in 1825 to prevent university buildings from being used for religious services that show without a doubt that he did *not* want religious services taking place on the campus.

Before the university actually opened, a request to hold a religious service in one of the finished pavilions was denied by the Board of Visitors. Because the *Rockfish Report* had specified only the Rotunda as a possible building in which religious services could be held, the board was able to fend off requests to hold religious services in other buildings by making it an unwritten policy to prohibit the use of university buildings for anything other than university purposes. Obviously, if Jefferson had really wanted religious services to be held at the university, he could easily have allowed them in another building until the Rotunda was finished. But he didn't. What he did was to use the wording of the *Rockfish Report* to avoid them as long as possible.

The board's building use policy was then invoked by Jefferson in April 1825, a month after the university opened, when the university's proctor, Arthur S. Brockenbrough, made a request to hold Sunday services in one of the pavilions. This was Jefferson's denial of that request:

In answer to your letter proposing to permit the lecturing room of the Pavilion No. 1. to be used regularly for prayers and preachings on Sundays, I have to observe that some 3. or 4. years ago, an application was made to permit a sermon to be preached in one of the pavilions on a particular occasion, not now recollected, it brought the subject into consideration with the Visitors, and altho they entered into no formal and written resolution on the occasion, the concurrent sentiment was that the buildings of the University belong to the state that they were erected for the purposes of an University, and that the Visitors, to whose care they are committed for those purposes have no right to permit their application to any other. and accordingly, when applied to, on the visit of General Lafayette, I declined at first the request of the use of the Rotunda for his entertainment, until it occurred on reflection that the room, in the unfinished state in which it then was, was as open and uninclosed, and as insusceptible of injury, as the field in which it stood. In the Rockfish report it was stated as probable that a building larger than the Pavilions might be called for in time, in which might be rooms for a library, for public examinations, and for religious worship under such impartial regulations as the Visitors should prescribe, the legislature neither sanctioned nor rejected this proposition; and afterwards, in the Report of Oct 1822, the board suggested, as a substitute, that the different religious sects should be invited to establish their separate theological schools in the vicinity of the University, in which the Students might attend religious worship, each in the form of his respective sect, and thus avoid all jealousy of attempts on his religious tenets. among the enactments of the board is one looking to this object, and superseding the first idea of permitting a room in the Rotunda to be used for religious worship, and of undertaking to frame a set of regulations of equality and impartiality among the multiplied sects.[80]

The sentence in this letter about allowing the use of the Rotunda for General Lafayette's dinner, which was added by Jefferson in the margin of his draft, isn't actually true. It appears that Jefferson realized after writing the rest of the letter that if he was going to use

80. Jefferson to Arthur S. Brockenbrough, April 21, 1825. *The Thomas Jefferson Papers, Series 1, General Correspondence, 1651-1827*, Library of Congress Manuscript Division.

the board's building policy to deny this request to hold religious services, he had to make up an excuse for allowing Lafayette's dinner, an event five months earlier that had clearly violated that policy. If anyone had wanted to question Jefferson's decision to deny the request to hold religious services, this dinner would have been their best argument, so Jefferson beat them to it and made it clear that bringing this up wasn't going to make him change his mind. Jefferson never denied a request to use the Rotunda for Lafayette's dinner. It was his idea to hold the dinner there.

Jefferson obviously didn't want his denial of this request to hold religious services to be made public, and was clearly relieved when Brockenbrough, who thought of publishing it in the local newspaper to be seen by the members of the local congregations who had asked him to make the request, wrote him this note asking for permission before doing so:

> With your permission I will publish in the Cent Gaz: your letter of the 21 April last seting forth your objections to permiting the lecture rooms of the Pav: to be used for prayer & reading on sundays your objections I have no doubt are perfectly satisfactory to all but the Bigoted part of the community and to correct any false statements that they may make, I wish it to go to the public [81]

This was Jefferson's reply to Brockenbrough:

> You have done very right in not publishing my letter of Apr. 21. I should have had immediately a whole kennel of Scriblers attacking me in the newspapers, insisting on their right to use a public building for any public exhibition, and drawing me into a paper war on the question. [82]

81. Draft of letter from Brockenbrough to Jefferson, written on the back of Jefferson's June 13, 1825 letter to Brockenbrough, Frank Edgar Grizzard, Jr., *Documentary History of the Construction of the Buildings at the University of Virginia, 1817–1828*, (Ph.D. Dissertation, University of Virginia, 1996).

82. Jefferson to Arthur S. Brockenbrough, June 20, 1825. *The Thomas Jefferson Papers, Series 1, General Correspondence, 1651-1827*, Library of Congress Manuscript Division.

What the "whole kennel of Scriblers" would have attacked Jefferson over was his claim that the proposal in the Board of Visitors' October 1822 report (the invitation to the religious sects) had superseded what the *Rockfish Report* said about religious worship in the Rotunda. Jefferson's claim in his letter to Brockenbrough that the 1822 invitation superseded the proposal in the *Rockfish Report* wasn't true.

The 1822 invitation didn't supersede what the *Rockfish Report* said about religious worship in the Rotunda. The 1822 invitation had actually allowed for the professors of the theological schools to use a room in the Rotunda for their lectures *because of* what the *Rockfish Report* said about religious worship in the Rotunda. And, the board's October 1824 report to the legislature, the last report before Jefferson's letter to Brockenbrough, had religious worship listed among the uses for the multi-purpose room in the Rotunda, as already described. The reason religious worship was included among the purposes of this room was, also *because of* what the *Rockfish Report* said about religious worship in the Rotunda. Both the 1822 and 1824 reports were written by Jefferson himself, so he obviously knew when he wrote his letter to Brockenbrough in April 1825 that nothing in the *Rockfish Report* had been superseded by the 1822 invitation. Jefferson just totally made this up to deny this 1825 request to hold religious services.

Jefferson's reason for his little fib when he denied this 1825 request to hold religious services isn't hard to figure out. None of the religious congregations in Charlottesville had a church in 1825. Four different denominations held their services in the courthouse, each getting one Sunday a month. This is why two of the congregations asked to use a building at the university. While the board's building policy could be used to deny requests for buildings other than the Rotunda, these same congregations would just make another request as soon as the Rotunda was completed – unless Jefferson gave them reason to believe that the part of the *Rockfish Report* allowing services in the Rotunda no longer applied. Apparently, this worked. None of the congregations requested to use the Rotunda when it was completed. As we'll see in the next section, it wasn't until 1828 that the first religious service was held in the Rotunda, and that wasn't because any of the congregations asked to use the building.

Contrary to all the evidence showing that Jefferson made a deliberate effort to prevent anything religious at his university, Barton once again claims that Jefferson took deliberate steps to promote religion there. Here's how he concludes this section:

> **Jefferson took many deliberate steps to ensure that religious instruction was an integral part of academic studies. Clearly, then, the claim that there was no Christian curriculum or instruction at the University of Virginia is demonstrably false and easily disproved by Jefferson's own writings.**

4. Did the University of Virginia Have Chaplains?

In this section Barton relies almost entirely on fudging the dates, using evidence from a much later date as if it were from the days of Jefferson. There were no chaplains or any other religious activity at the university while Jefferson was alive, and nothing while James Madison was in charge that wouldn't be allowed in today's public schools. But Barton, as usual, doesn't let pesky details like dates stand in the way of his version of history.

Barton begins the section:

The modern claim that the University of Virginia had no chaplains is also easily disproved by original documents, including early newspaper ads that the University ran to recruit students from surrounding areas.

Barton then proceeds to present a few of these "early newspaper ads that the University ran." The problem is that they aren't early enough. But Barton's readers won't know that unless they look up his footnotes for them, which is what he counts on them not doing. By not providing the dates in the text of the book, his readers will assume that by "early" he means when the university was first founded by Jefferson.

The first ad that Barton presents is actually a letter from the chaplain of the university, Rev. Septimus Huston, that ran in the

Washington Globe. But this ad is from 1837, eleven years after Jefferson died.

A university ad being written by a chaplain at this time is no big mystery. This was still in the time period when writers were bashing Jefferson and the university for being irreligious. People were reading things like the review of George Tucker's Jefferson biography that we looked at in a previous section. That also came out 1837, and was typical of what was being written about Jefferson at the time. Obviously, things like that book review in a religious publication might keep religious students away from the university. An ad written by the chaplain would tell those people that the university wasn't completely irreligious. The university did have a chaplain, paid for with private contributions from the students and faculty who wanted to have a chaplain, and did have regular religious services. These things didn't exist when Jefferson was alive, but they did in 1837.

What's interesting is what Barton *omits* when quoting what this university chaplain wrote in this ad. Yes, Barton actually has to edit what a chaplain at the university wrote because it conflicts with his version of the history of the university. For example, the chaplain said that the university had invited the various religious denominations to open their own theological schools. Barton leaves that part in. But the chaplain also said that none of the denominations accepted the invitation. Barton cuts that part out because it would conflict with his earlier lies that require these theological schools to have actually existed.

Barton also edits out anything indicating that what religious instruction there was at the university wasn't part of the university's curriculum. The chaplain said that religious instruction consisted of a weekly lecture that alternated between the houses of two professors and a Sabbath school "in which several of the pious students are engaged." Obviously, that contradicts Barton's claims of all that religious instruction in the university's curriculum, so he just edits the part about the religious lectures and Sabbath school out.

But the main problem, of course, is that this ad was from eleven years after Jefferson's death, so the fact that there was a chaplain at that time has absolutely nothing to do with Jefferson.

The next ad Barton quotes is from even later. This one is from 1843, seventeen years after Jefferson's death:

> **Religious services are regularly performed at the University by a *chaplain*, who is appointed in turn from the four principal denominations of the state. And by a resolution of the faculty, *ministers of the gospel and young men preparing for the ministry may attend any of the schools without payment of fees to the professors*. (Emphasis added)**

Barton then gives his explanation of this 1843 ad:

> **It was the custom of the day that university faculty members receive their salaries from fees paid by the students directly to the staff, but the university waived those fees for students studying for the Gospel ministry. So, if the school was secular, as claimed by so many of today's writers, then why did it extend *preferential* treatment to students pursuing religious careers? Surely a truly secular University would have given preference to students who were not religiously oriented.**

Barton has things a bit mixed up here. The university itself did not extend any preferential treatment to ministers and ministry students. This was not a university policy. It was only a resolution of the faculty, by which the professors waived their own fees.

This practice (begun in 1841, fifteen years after Jefferson's death) did not exempt ministers and ministry students from the fees of the university itself. This is how it appeared in the "Expenses," not the "Regulations," section of the 1841 university catalog:

> Ministers of the Gospel, and young men preparing for the ministry, may attend any of the schools of the University, without payment of fees to the Professors. [83]

---

83. *University of Virginia Catalog*, 1841, 18.

167

An ad for the university in an 1845 magazine clearly stated that this was only a resolution of the faculty:

> And by a resolution of the faculty, ministers of the Gospel may attend any of the schools, without the payment of fees to the professors. The same privilege is extended to young men who are preparing for the ministry, upon their presenting to the Faculty satisfactory evidence of decided merit. [84]

But once again, of course, we're talking about something that had absolutely nothing to do with Jefferson since it didn't begin until 1841. And, once again, Barton does not make it clear that this didn't happen until long after Jefferson was gone, referring to the practice of professors being paid directly by the students only as "the custom of that day," and not saying in his text that what he's quoting is from 1843.

Barton then gets to the subject of chaplains, coming up with the following excuse for why there were no chaplains at the university when Jefferson was there:

> **The University of Virginia did indeed have chaplains, albeit not in its first three years (the University opened for students in 1825). At the beginning, when the university was establishing its reputation as a transdenominational university, the school had no appointed chaplain for the same reason that there had been no clergyman as president and no single professor of divinity: an ordained clergyman in any of those three positions might send an incorrect signal that the University was aligned with a specific denomination.**

So, we're back to the whole "transdenominational" thing again. Nowhere and at no time did Jefferson ever write or do anything that

---

84. Advertisement for the University of Virginia, *Southern Literary Messenger,* Vol. XI, Issue 12, December 1845.

could possibly be construed as anything like what Barton claims to be the reason for not having chaplains or other members of the clergy at the university. Barton needs to explain away why the university had no chaplain under Jefferson, so he uses this catch-all transdenominational thing that he made up at the beginning of his chapter.

For his next lie, Barton completely misquotes and takes out of context something written by James Madison:

But by 1829, when the nondenominational reputation of the university had been fully established, President Madison (who became rector of the University after Jefferson's death in 1826) announced "that [permanent] provision for religious instruction and observance among the students would be made by... services of clergymen."

First of all, Madison did not "announce" anything about religious instruction or the services of clergymen. What Barton is (mis)quoting here is from an 1827 letter that Madison wrote to one of the other university board members who had opposed Jefferson's policy of barring clergymen as professors and wanted the replacement for a professor who was resigning to be a clergyman.

Although a complete disregard of Jefferson's policies regarding religion didn't really begin to take hold until the 1840s, the first signs of what was to come began within two years of Jefferson's death. When George Long, the Professor of Natural Philosophy, announced in 1827 that he planned to resign, Chapman Johnson, who had always opposed Jefferson's exclusion of clergymen, made it clear that he wanted Long's replacement to be a clergyman. But, even with Jefferson gone, Johnson knew he would have to get either Joseph Cabell or James Madison to go along, so he wrote to John Hartwell Cocke, the other board member he knew would side with him, and asked him to work on Cabell. This is from Johnson's letter:

Tell Cabell...it is time to give up his old prejudice upon this subject, the offspring of the French Revolution, long since

a bastard by a divorce of the unnatural alliance between
liberty and atheism.[85]

What? Chapman Johnson, an original member of Jefferson's
Board of Visitors, thought that Jefferson's policies were the offspring
of the atheism of France? He didn't understand that Jefferson only
instituted these policies because he was trying to create a transdenominational university? Too bad David Barton wasn't around
back then to explain this to the university's board.

Chapman Johnson also wrote to Madison, apparently trying to
trick him into stating his position on hiring clergymen by claiming
that he had reason to *suspect* that a particular candidate for the
professorship might be a clergyman. Madison didn't buy this, and
didn't give Johnson a definite answer. What Madison did was to list
all the problems that allowing clergymen into the professorships
could cause. Madison was fully aware that Johnson was scheming to
bring religion into the university by putting clergymen on the faculty,
so he ended his letter by making it absolutely clear that he wanted
religious worship and instruction to be initiated by the students,
not the university.

This is the part of Madison's 1828 letter to Chapman Johnson
that Barton creates his misquote from:

> I have indulged more particularly the hope, that provision
> for religious instruction & observances among the Stu-
> dents, would be made by themselves or their parents &
> guardians, each contributing to a fund, to be applied in
> remunerating the services of Clergymen of denomina-
> tions corresponding with the preference of Contributors.
> Small contributions would suffice, and the arrangements
> would become more adequate and more efficient as the
> Students become more numerous, whilst being altogether
> voluntary, it would interfere neither with the characteristic

85. Philip Alexander Bruce, *History of the University of Virginia 1818-1819*, vol. 2, (New
York: The Macmillan Company, 1920), 150.

peculiarity of the University, the consecrated principle of
the law, nor the spirit of the Country. [86]

Then, based on his misquote of Madison's letter, which he
claims was something that Madison "announced" as some sort of
policy regarding chaplains, Barton continues:

**The University therefore extended official recognition to
one primary chaplain for all the students, with the chaplain
position rotating annually among the major denominations
that Jefferson identified as the Baptists, Methodists, Presbyterians, and Anglicans. In 1829 Presbyterian clergyman
Rev. Edward Smith became the first chaplain of the University of Virginia. It was an official University position – but
unpaid. In 1833, after three-fourths of the students pledged
their own money for the chaplain's support, Methodist
William Hammett became the first paid chaplain. He led
Sunday worship and daily morning prayer meetings in the
Rotunda. In 1855 the University built a parsonage to provide a residence for the University chaplain. ... Clearly, the
University of Virginia *did* have chaplains.**

Well, this all certainly sounds like the university, under James
Madison, created an official university position for a chaplain in
1829. But look at the three dates Barton gives – 1829, 1833, and
1855. These dates give the impression of continuity, but are actually because of a lack of continuity.

The reason that a parsonage for the chaplain wasn't built until
1855 was because the Board of Visitors under Madison wouldn't
even allow a chaplain to live on the campus, let alone build a parsonage for them. The board considered providing a residence for a
chaplain on government property to be pecuniary support of religion, even if that chaplain was paid for with private donations from

---

86. James Madison to Chapman Johnson, May 1, 1828. *The James Madison Papers at the
Library of Congress, Series 1, General Correspondence,* Library of Congress Manuscript
Division.

students and faculty members. That's the reason the parsonage wasn't built until 1855.

By saying that the first chaplain at the university was in 1829, and then jumping to the chaplain who was hired with private donations in 1833, Barton gives the impression that there was also a chaplain between 1829 and 1833. There wasn't, and the reason there wasn't was the policy prohibiting chaplains from living on the campus. The students couldn't come up with enough money to hire a chaplain because the chaplain's salary had to be high enough to cover not only their duties as a chaplain but also the rental of an off-campus place to live in Charlottesville. Obviously, if James Madison had been in favor of having a chaplain at the university, he could easily have just changed the policy and allowed the chaplain to live on the campus. But he didn't. He left the students in a position where they couldn't afford to have a chaplain.

It wasn't until 1833 that the students were able to raise enough money to hire the first chaplain since 1829. It wasn't three-fourths of the students as Barton claims it was, but some of the students did sign a pledge to contribute towards hiring a chaplain. This pledge was the doing of one particularly religious student.

What Madison described in that 1828 letter to Chapman Johnson that Barton gets his earlier misquote from is exactly what eventually did happen. During the 1832-1833 school year, a student named McClurg Wickham took charge and organized a group of about thirty students, all of whom signed a pledge that between them they would contribute enough money to pay the salary of a chaplain. Wickham's plan was approved by the chairman of the faculty and presented to the Board of Visitors, who approved it at their July 1833 meeting. Members of the faculty and the board also contributed to the students' chaplain fund, but strictly as individuals in a private capacity.

In addition to hiring a chaplain, Wickham wanted to start a Sunday school, and requested the use of the room in the Rotunda for his classes. This request was denied by the chairman of the faculty, who thought it went beyond what was allowed by both the *Rockfish Report*, which allowed the use of the room for worship services, and the board's 1822 invitation to the religious sects, which allowed for teachers from the various religious schools that didn't exist to use the room in the Rotunda for lectures. The Board of Visitors, however, did decide to allow Wickham the use of a room in one of the pavilions.

Interestingly, with its decision to allow this student-run religious group the use of a room in one of the pavilions, the university's board did in the 1830s exactly what is required in today's public schools. Other student groups at the university, such as debating and academic societies, had been allowed the use of rooms in the pavilions and in the basement of the Rotunda, so denying the same privilege to another group of students simply because their activities were religious would be considered unconstitutional by today's standards. So, what the modern Supreme Court has ruled is exactly what James Madison, the "Father of the Constitution," decided way back in the 1830s.

As I've said in previous sections of this book, the big push for a religious takeover of the university began after both Jefferson and Madison were gone, beginning in the late 1830s and in full swing by the 1840s. The clergy and others of that time who did not support Jefferson's secular policies didn't lie about them; they acknowledged that Jefferson founded a completely secular university, said that they thought Jefferson was wrong to found a completely secular university, and set out to change his secular policies.

The following excerpts from an article in the January 1842 issue of the *Southern Literary Messenger* are typical of what was being written about the university at the time that its religifying was getting underway:

> Experiment has proved that Mr. Jefferson committed one great error[87] in the system of government which he sought to establish in the University. But this was as the dust of the balance to that of banishing religion from her walls. The whole should have been planned and exe-

87. i.e., the omission of a Department of English Literature.

cuted in reliance upon Divine aid and direction; for nothing can be truer than except the Lord build the house, they labor in vain who build it. Without being superstitious, the overruling hand of Providence must be acknowledged; and apprehensions sometimes arise lest Heaven has decreed the fall of the University, in order to prove to man the folly and impiety of founding such institutions, without invoking its blessing. Religion cannot be safely separated from any human undertaking. For literature and science to produce their salutary effects upon the mind and heart – to make man better as they make him wiser – they must be associated with, and tempered by, religion; nor should their connection be slight and incidental, but designed and intimate. The system of Mr. Jefferson has been abandoned; and there are now regular religious services twice a week, and the students pay marked respect to the minister. But the fact of having a chaplain is a small matter. He must not be looked upon as a mere preacher and sermonizer on Sundays, but as pastor and instructor in religious matters; not as a mere appendage, but as an important, an essential part of the institution. Religion must be admitted, not as a secondary matter, but as of primary concern; not as an incident, but an essential; not through complaisance to public opinion, to allay the fears of anxious parents, nor as a compromise between the opposition of Mr. Jefferson, and the convictions of the Visiters....

...The first thing to be done is to erect a suitable chapel. The faculty are anxious for this to be effected, and presented a memorial to the Visiters on the subject. At the request of the writer, Professor Bonnycastle drew up an eloquent memorial to be presented on the part of the students; but as circumstances prevented the signatures from being obtained, it was not handed in. A chapel is not only necessary for the religious services, but for public occasions, anniversary orations, the use of societies, and for important meetings of the students, when they wish to do honor to the memory of a departed fellow-student or professor. It will also be useful as an ornament, and this dreadful hiatus, so painfully obvious to every Christian friend of the institution, should be speedily supplied....[88]

As this article indicates, by 1842, there had already been some increase in religious activity at the university, but not enough to satisfy everyone. Almost as soon as Madison retired, the board began to relax some of the rules. The very first school year that he wasn't there, the chaplain was allowed to live on the campus. By 1840, with a number of new professors who opposed the university's secular policies, conditions were right for an all-out campaign to make religion an integral part of the university. One of the new professors was James Lawrence Cabell, a nephew of Joseph C. Cabell, hired in 1837 as Professor of Anatomy. James Cabell was a leader in the movement to build a chapel and parsonage at the university, and also began leading a weekly Bible study. And, just as Jefferson had predicted two decades earlier, it would be the Presbyterians who would attempt to establish their particular brand of religion at the university as soon as an opportunity presented itself. James W. Alexander, a Presbyterian minister, and brother-in-law of James Lawrence Cabell, noted the progression of religion at the university in several of his letters to fellow Presbyterian minister John Hall.

In 1840, when it was really beginning to look like a complete religious takeover might be possible, Alexander wrote to Hall:

The religious prospects of the University of Virginia are really encouraging. It seems as if Providence was throwing contempt on old Jefferson's ashes.[89]

88. "The University of Virginia," *Southern Literary Messenger,* Vol. VIII, Issue 1, January 1842, 53-54.
89. James W. Alexander to John Hall, June 10, 1840. John Hall, D.D., ed., *Forty Years' Familiar Letters of James W. Alexander, D.D.,* vol. 1, (New York: Charles Scribner, 1860), 305.

In another letter to Hall, after visiting the university seven years later, Alexander wrote:

> Jefferson knew how to select one of the finest plateaus in the land for this college. His antichristian plans have been singularly thwarted in every way. For example, here is a chapel, (since I was here last;) three professors are communicants, besides Dr. McGuffey, who is a Presbyterian minister; and a proctor and treasurer who are Presbyterian communicants. McGuffey is a West Pennsylvanian, and is second to no man in Virginia for fame as a lecturer and public speaker. He does not preach here, but often in other places. I shall not be surprised if, before ten years, this rich and central institution should have on its very grounds a Presbyterian theological school; as the law founding the university gives leave to any Christian sect to build, and to have a theological professor, with freedom of library, apparatus, &c....[90]

Alexander's reference in this 1847 letter to a chapel does not mean that an actual chapel had been built. What Alexander was referring to was a lecturing room in one of the wings of the Rotunda, which had been designated for religious worship in 1841. The Rotunda's wings, originally intended as gymnasiums, turned out not to be well suited for that purpose. In the mid-1830s, the board decided to divide the wings into lecturing rooms. Because the school had grown, the lecturing room in which the first religious services were held had become too small. The larger room that the services were moved to, which unlike the old room was designated solely for religious worship rather than being a multi-purpose room that could be used for religious worship, was the "chapel" until an actual chapel was built in the late 1880s.

Although Rev. Alexander seemed to consider the lecturing room

---

90. James W. Alexander to John Hall, May 27, 1847. John Hall, D.D., ed., *Forty Years' Familiar Letters of James W. Alexander, D.D.*, vol. 2, (New York: Charles Scribner, 1860), 71.

"chapel" a significant improvement, the author of the 1842 *Southern Literary Messenger* article certainly didn't find it adequate:

> In the university, the services are performed in the lecture-room, which is very inconveniently arranged, and where the mind is diverted by a thousand perceptions and associations. Every thing in connection with the *spirituel* of that institution would show, if we did not know the fact, that the introduction of religion was an afterthought. In all her extensive arrangements, there is not a single accommodation for religion. [91]

Barton concludes this section, and his argument that Jefferson didn't found a secular university, with this:

> **In short, first-hand source documents, especially Jefferson's own writings, incontestably refute all four modern assertions about the alleged secular nature of the University of Virginia. If anyone examines the original sources and claims otherwise, they are, to use the words of early military chaplain William Peter Wolf, just as likely to "look all over the sky at high noon on a cloudless day and not see the sun."**

Well, Mr. Barton, I *have* examined the original sources and I claim otherwise – and I can see the sun just fine.

---

91. "The University of Virginia," *Southern Literary Messenger,* Vol. VIII, Issue 1, January 1842, 54.

Question With Boldness
Even the Existence of a God

Awkwardly tagged onto the end of Barton's chapter on Jefferson and the University of Virginia is a nine page section on a letter made famous among his followers by his buddy and promoter Glenn Beck. Over the past few years, Beck has made a particular line from this letter his motto, and Barton apparently finds Beck's incessant repeating of this line to their mutual followers inconvenient enough to feel the need to address it. Beck's motto, from a 1787 letter Jefferson wrote to his nephew Peter Carr, is:

"Question with boldness even the existence of a god."

Peter Carr was studying under Jefferson's own former teacher, George Wythe, one of the three men whom Jefferson credited with turning his life around over two decades earlier. In April 1787, Carr wrote the following to his uncle about what Wythe was teaching him:

I am still at the university attending the professors of Nat. and Mor. philosophy, Mathematicks and modern languages; and Mr. Wythe has given me a very friendly invitation to his lectures on law. I have likewise the good fortune to be a private pupil, and am now reading with him, Herodotus, Sophocles, Cicero and some particular

179

parts of Horace. Beside the advantage of his literary instructions he adds advice and lessons of morality, which are not only pleasing and instructive now, but will be (I hope) of real utility in future. He is said to be without religion, but to me he appears to possess the most rational part of it, and fulfills that great command, Do unto all men as thou wouldst they should do unto thee. And now Sir I should be glad of your advice on the subject of religion; as I think it time to be fixed on a point which has had so many advocates and opponents, and still seems to be dubious. I should wish your advice as to the books I should read, and in what order. Mr. Wythe has just put Lucretius into my hands, whose sect and opinions, men generally think dangerous, but under so good a guide I fear not his opinions whatever they be, and hope rather to be benefited, than as some scrupulous people think, contaminated by him.[92]

Barton goes through pages of gymnastics to explain away what Jefferson wrote to his nephew, claiming that Jefferson was "actually instructing Peter in apologetics." And, why was Jefferson instructing his nephew in apologetics? Why, because of that Scottish Common Sense philosophy, of course!

> **Recall that Jefferson's own education took the Scottish Common Sense approach. It attacked European skepticism, praised the compatibility of reason and revelation, and demonstrated the superiority of evidence in all challenges. Jefferson had been trained in this vein of apologetics and it was in that same spirit that he challenged Peter to question – that is, to examine – the evidence of God's existence. In light of this background, consider the now infamous section from Jefferson's letter.**

So, yes, by all means, please do consider the infamous section

---

92. Peter Carr to Jefferson, April 18, 1787. Julian P. Boyd, ed., *The Papers of Thomas Jefferson*, vol. 11, (Princeton, NJ: Princeton University Press, 1955), 299.

of Jefferson's letter. Here's the entire section. Make up your own mind about it.

Religion. Your reason is now mature enough to examine this object. In the first place divest yourself of all bias in favour of novelty & singularity of opinion. Indulge them in any other subject rather than that of religion. It is too important, & the consequences of error may be too serious. On the other hand shake off all the fears & servile prejudices under which weak minds are servilely crouched. Fix reason firmly in her seat, and call to her tribunal every fact, every opinion. Question with boldness even the existence of a god; because, if there be one, he must more approve of the homage of reason, than that of blindfolded fear. You will naturally examine first the religion of your own country. Read the bible then, as you would read Livy or Tacitus. The facts which are within the ordinary course of nature you will believe on the authority of the writer, as you do those of the same kind in Livy & Tacitus. The testimony of the writer weighs in their favor in one scale, and their not being against the laws of nature does not weigh against them. But those facts in the bible which contradict the laws of nature, must be examined with more care, and under a variety of faces. Here you must recur to the pretensions of the writer to inspiration from god. Examine upon what evidence his pretensions are founded, and whether that evidence is so strong as that its falsehood would be more improbable than a change in the laws of nature in the case he relates. For example in the book of Joshua we are told the sun stood still several hours. Were we to read that fact in Livy or Tacitus we should class it with their showers of blood, speaking of statues, beasts, &c. But it is said that the writer of that book was inspired. Examine therefore candidly what evidence there is of his having been inspired. The pretension is entitled to your inquiry, because millions believe it. On the other hand you are astronomer enough to know how contrary it is to the law of nature that a body revolving on its axis as the earth does, should have stopped, should not by that sudden stoppage have prostrated animals, trees, buildings, and should after a certain time have resumed its revolution, & that without a second general prostration. Is this arrest of the earth's motion, or the evidence which affirms it, most within the law of probabilities? You will next read the new testament. It is the history of a personage called Jesus. Keep in your eye the opposite pretensions 1. of those who say he was begotten by god, born of a virgin, suspended & reversed the laws of nature at will, & ascended bodily into heaven: and 2. of those who say he was a man of illegitimate birth, of a benevolent heart, enthusiastic mind, who set out without pretensions to divinity, ended in believing them, & was punished capitally for sedition by being gibbeted according to the Roman law which punished the first commission of that offence by whipping, & the second by exile or death in furcâ. See this law in the Digest Lib. 48. tit. 19. §. 28. 3. & Lipsius Lib. 2. de cruce. cap. 2. These questions are examined in the books I have mentioned under the head of religion, & several others. They will assist you in your inquiries, but keep your reason firmly on the watch in reading them all. Do not be frightened from this inquiry by any fear of it's consequences. If it ends in a belief that there is no god, you will find incitements to virtue in the comfort & pleasantness you feel in it's exercise, and the love of others which it will procure you. If you find reason to believe there is a god, a consciousness that you are acting under his eye, & that he approves you, will be a vast additional incitement; if that there be a future state, the hope of a happy existence in that increases the appetite to deserve it; if that Jesus was also a god, you will be comforted by a belief of his aid and love. In fine, I repeat that you must lay aside all prejudice on both sides, & neither believe nor reject anything because any other persons, or description of persons have rejected or believed it. Your own reason is the only oracle given you by heaven, and you are answerable not for the rightness but uprightness of the decision. I forgot to observe when speaking of the new testament that you should read all the histories of Christ, as well of those whom a council of ecclesiastics have decided for us to be Pseudo-evangelists, as those they named Evangelists. Because these Pseudo-evangelists pretended to inspiration as much as the

others, and you are to judge their pretensions by your own reason, & not by the reason of those ecclesiastics. Most of these are
lost. There are some however still extant, collected by Fabricius
which I will endeavor to get & send you.[93]

93. Jefferson to Peter Carr, August 10, 1787. Paul Leicester Ford, ed., *The Works of
Thomas Jefferson,* vol. 5, (New York: G.P. Putnam's Sons, 1904), 324-327.

29308414R00108

Made in the USA
Middletown, DE
14 February 2016